D0177967

79 676 460 5

A TOMMY IN THE FAMILY

A
TOMMY
IN THE
FAMILY

FIRST WORLD WAR FAMILY
HISTORY AND RESEARCH

KEITH GREGSON

The History Press

First published 2014

The History Press
The Mill, Brimscombe Port
Stroud, Gloucestershire, GL5 2QG
www.thehistorypress.co.uk

British Library Cataloguing in Publication Data.
A catalogue record for this book is available from the British Library.

ISBN 978 0 7524 9336 7

Typesetting and origination by The History Press
Printed in Great Britain

CONTENTS

Introduction 7

The First World War: A Very Brief Synopsis 14

1 Fred 'Pop' Stephens: A Sapper's Tale 18

2 John Stephens: A Prisoner of War's Tale 33

3 Lil Stephens: Tale of a POW's Wife 47

4 Charles Stephens (1888–1972):
Tale from a 'Forgotten Front' 55

5 Hal Gregson: 'Flyer's Tale' 62

6 Billy Gregson: Tales from a Raconteur 69

7 Joe Bentley: A Mysterious Tale 76

8 Joe Greatorex (1891–1980): A Casualty's Tale 83

9 Gert Greatorex: The Tale of a Casualty's Wife 94

10 Janet Dawson: The Tale of an Army Nurse 103

11 William Thomas: Tale of a Trench Raid 110

12 Ernest Bridge (1896–1915) and Norman
Bridge (1897–1918): A Tale of Lost Brothers 118

13 Fred Monk: A Tale Unravelled 125

14 Cyril Monk (1899–1917): The Tale of a Precious Son 133

15 Frederick James Sleath: The Tale of a Sniper Officer 138

16 Reginald Banyard: A Truly Remarkable Tale 150

17 Hughie Cairns: A Footballer's Tale 162

18	Tom Crawford: An Entertainer's Tale	169
19	Artie Watterson: A Submariner's Tale	176
20	Wilkinson, Lucas, Tiddy and Butterworth:	
	The Morris Dancers' Tale	182

Index | 189

INTRODUCTION

When I was a youngster in the late 1950s and early 1960s my father, who was a lay reader in the Church of England, would often take the Remembrance Day service at the local cenotaph. The old men who marched past the memorial proudly and stiffly were mostly veterans of the First World War, or the Great War as it was still known to some, despite a second global conflict. One or two were even survivors of the earlier Boer War. You saw them around the town day in day out. Some, it was said, never talked about their experiences 'in the trenches' except when in the company of others who had had a similar experience. Now they are all gone and we are left with memories some of them shared with members of my generation (now approaching old age themselves), and a mass of documentation in public and private hands. The tales which follow draw on these different types of primary evidence.

The main aim of the book is to expose as many ways as possible of discovering ancestral information concerning the First World War. Like one of my previous History Press publications, *A Viking In The Family and Other Family Tree Tales*, the book draws on a number of case studies put together with the help of family and friends. During my thirty-three years as a classroom teacher of history, the First World War featured large in a number of the courses I taught and I was fortunate enough to become a magnet for primary source material kindly donated by a variety

The author's father taking Remembrance Day service, Carlisle 1960s.

of people. I used this material in the classroom, in most cases in its original form, and it was treated with the utmost respect, even awe, by the pupils. It was quite something for a youngster to handle a battered notebook which had been in the breast pocket of a soldier throughout the Somme campaign.

The main source for this book lies in my own family and here I am in the fairly unique position of having access to the war diaries of three brothers: my maternal grandfather and two great-uncles. The diaries featured briefly in the *Viking* book and it is a thrilling experience to be able to explore their contents in more detail here. My grandfather, Fred 'Pop' Stephens (chapter one), served in the Royal Engineers from 1915–19 and saw active service in Gallipoli; he was also present during a number of other major campaigns which were fought out along the Western Front. His various notebooks were transcribed by 'Pop' himself into a single school exercise book immediately on his return.

This is in my possession along with his medals and an assortment of other useful and informative memorabilia.

Fred's older brother John (chapter two) was in the King's Liverpool Regiment and was captured in the German offensive of 1918. He kept detailed diaries of his experiences as a prisoner of war. These were transcribed by his daughter, the late Joan Shrewsbury (*née* Stephens). I have seen the originals and have a copy of the transcription as well as other original documents and memorabilia relating to his experiences. Among the documents are many connected to John's wife Lil (chapter three) and her efforts to discover what had happened to her husband after he was reported missing. It has thus been possible to tell her story too.

Charles or Charlie (chapter four), the youngest of the three brothers, kept the most detailed of the diaries. He was sent to India to 'defend the Empire' from attacks from within and without. Although he and his comrades did not see the type of action usually associated with the First World War, all was far from plain sailing, as the diaries reveal.

All three brothers survived the war, as witnessed by a moving photograph taken in the family backyard in Millom, Cumberland in 1919.

My mother recalls that my great-grandmother took the boys' uniforms, tore them into strips and made a traditional northern 'clippie' mat out of them. The mat disintegrated many years ago.

My paternal grandfather, Harold 'Hal' Gregson (chapter five), served most of the war in the Royal Flying Corps/Royal Air Force and was nicknamed 'Flyer'. From the bits and pieces we have gleaned on him has come a tale as amusing as it is informative. His brother 'Billy' (chapter six), who featured in the *Viking* book for reasons other than those concerning the First World War, was a great storyteller and part of the research here has been to see if the truth of his tales can be verified.

Fred, John and Charlie, Devonshire Road, Millom, Cumberland 1919.

My father's only sibling, Geoff, married in 1952 and died of tuberculosis soon after. His wife, Anne, died in 2011 and left behind a suitcase of photographs connected to her family. Among these was a series of pictures which allowed me to put together the remarkable story of her young great-uncle Joe who, as it turned out, lost his life in an action which for many years after the event provided one of the great mysteries of the war (chapter seven).

One fortunate outcome of my First World War interest was that I was left the First World War material belonging to my paternal grandmother's brother T.J. 'Joe' Greatorex (chapter eight). Joe was a gamekeeper by profession, a crack-shot and, later in life, an internationally respected gun-dog breeder. He saw active service, fell ill on the front and later became a Lewis gun instructor. He kept all his main official war documents as well as letters written from hospital, both at the front and in England. As with the cases of John and Lil Stephens (chapters two and three), these documents enable us to tell the tale of the one who was left at home, in this case Joe's wife Gert (*née* Evans) (chapter nine).

Nor do my immediate family case studies stop here. Partly as a consequence of the First World War, my maternal grandfather 'Pop' Stephens married twice. My natural grandmother died of cancer in 1932, leaving my grandfather with my mother as a ten-year-old. In the 1930s he married Janet Thomas (*née* Dawson) (chapter ten), a childhood friend, who was widowed and also had a young daughter. She had nursed and married a South African war hero, William Thomas (chapter eleven). He served in East Africa, was wounded twice on the Western Front and died in the 1920s as a result of weakness caused by his war wounds. Janet was present at one of the great home-based military disasters of the war and also left me all the fascinating material relating to her first husband's medal-winning war activities. Her individual tale concerning the Gretna Rail Tragedy of 1915 featured in the *Viking* book and is touched on again briefly here.

As far as I know, all my blood relatives survived the war. This was not the case with my wife's family. Her paternal grandmother Grace Monk (*née* Bridge) was one of the six children of an Essex village shopkeeper. There were four girls and two boys in the family. The girls lived to a ripe old age; the boys Ernest and Norman (jointly appearing in chapter twelve) were both killed on the Western Front.

My wife's paternal grandfather, Fred Monk (chapter thirteen), went late to the war, served briefly on the Italian Front and, like John Stephens (chapter two), was captured on the Western Front during the German advance of 1918. It was said that he never talked of his experiences but I discovered otherwise. His youngest brother Cyril, apple of his mother's eye and hope of the family in academic terms, went to war as a teenager and was never seen again (chapter fourteen).

Acquaintances of my late father have provided me with further material of use and interest. Material left in the attic of their 'White Elephant Shop' in Carlisle included the wartime memorabilia of Reg Banyard (chapter fifteen). He had been a sapper on the Somme and his pocketbook, used for numerous purposes while in the trenches, is a real gem, coming up with one of the most moving pieces of evidence war can throw up. Similarly material relating to a Fred Sleath (chapter sixteen) was discovered in the attic. He had been an officer and responsible, according to his own literature, for setting up one of the first sniping sections on the Western Front. This he did in the early part of the war before moving into Intelligence. He left the type-written script for a book based on his experiences, which gives a remarkable insight into the 'art' of sniping.

Early in the twenty-first century, I was asked in my capacity as a musician and singer-songwriter to judge a songwriting competition at a folk-related gathering in Northumberland. One of the winning entries was about a young Northumbrian footballer who had moved to Canada just before the war and had been awarded a posthumous Victoria Cross. I decided to follow up the story of Hughie Cairns (chapter seventeen) in detail and it proved a very worthwhile exercise. Tom Crawford (chapter eighteen) was a retired music hall and seaside promenade entertainer whom my father met in later life. When Tom died, he left his memorabilia to my father and this included information on his service in the Royal Flying Corps during the war.

Another remarkable tale has come as a result of a marriage into the family. At my nephew's wedding I engaged in lengthy conversation with the bride's aunt, Alison Harris. She had done some tremendous research into an ancestor who had served in submarines in the First World War. It is a tale with a tragic ending and one worth the telling (chapter nineteen).

The last story is one I was keen to include for personal reasons. A lifelong love of morris dancing (a much derided pastime) has led me to tell the moving and tragic tale of a group of distinguished dancers who paid the ultimate price while serving their country, the traditions of which they all held dear (chapter twenty).

As to the book's title, 'Tommy' or 'Tommy Atkins' was the generic term used for the British soldier. Though some of the case studies in this book are not directly related to true 'Tommies', the general title remains attractive enough, while widening the content to include 'non-Tommies' ought to provide assistance to those researching family experience in the First World War. Hopefully these case studies, the stories behind them, and the accompanying tips will combine to make *A Tommy in the Family* both interesting and helpful to such researchers.

My thanks go to my family and all who have supported and helped me in this venture. They will be referred to in detail in the main text although, as ever, the ultimate responsibility for the work is my own.

Keith Gregson
Sunderland
2013

THE FIRST WORLD WAR: A VERY BRIEF SYNOPSIS

After over thirty years at the chalkface of history (and some brief respite thereafter), I find it an interesting not to say challenging exercise to sit back and summarise briefly a topic which occupied so much time and space during those working years. Here then is the result.

It has become easier with the passage of time to look back and appreciate the various causes of the war and also the fact that for years this particular war had been 'an accident waiting to happen'. Most of the countries involved from the early stages including Britain, France, Germany, Austria, Italy and Russia carry some of the blame; all were pushed by the fashion of the times to expand their borders and/or the borders of dependent territories. The war started in July/August 1914 mainly because the timing suited the war plans of the German/Austrian alliance, which were based on the certainty that they would have to fight the other three (France, Russia and Britain) on a variety of fronts. The guns were silenced in November 1918 chiefly on account of the narrow failure of a last German victory push in Western Europe earlier in April. This failure allowed the entry of the relatively fresh and well-armed USA into the war (1917) to be decisive.

The men who served in the British and Commonwealth (Empire) forces between 1914 and 1918 did so as regulars, volunteers and conscripts. They were in the Royal Navy and the army (including its Royal Flying Corps (RFC) which took on its role as a separate third force – the Royal Air Force (RAF) – during this very war). For some, regulars and recruits alike, their war started on the very first day, 4 August 1914. For others, because of age and/or method of 'joining up', the war was shorter, in some cases lasting only a matter of weeks or months.

On land, soldiers, airmen and even, on occasion, sailors, served on a number of fronts. The most famous of these was the Western Front, a moveable front which at one point famously stretched from Switzerland to the North Sea. The front lines (still known as 'The Trenches' today), were often separated by less than a few hundred yards in places. They settled down where they were in France and Belgium because the initial German push into France had been repelled in 1914 along the River Marne. The retreating Germans had then been ordered to 'down anchor' and battle it out (i.e. they were pushed back 'onto' the River Marne - not 'into' it, as one of my pupils once wrote). These lines moved backwards and forwards over the following four years but in general terms very little ground was gained by either side. Behind these front lines developed a maze of supporting trenches and tunnels and transport systems. This system, developed through stalemate between the two sides, was in place for all but the first few months of the war and naturally features heavily in this book.

There was also an Eastern Front across on the Russian western border but troops from Britain and the Commonwealth had little involvement with campaigns here, although members of the Royal and Merchant Navy did support the Russians in the Baltic. Fighting also took place in the Italian Alps. This involved British and Commonwealth troops at times, sent to support their Italian allies.

Perhaps the best known of the other fronts or sideshows from the British and Commonwealth point of view was the Gallipoli or Dardanelles campaign of 1915. Here the aim, according to Churchill, was to start an attack on the 'soft underbelly of Europe' by taking the peninsula from the Turkish allies of the Germans. This would allow troops to march north against the weak south of Austria and also for the navy to go through the Dardanelles and communicate with Russian allies by sea to the south. The campaign, which lasted from April 1915 to January 1916 and featured many ANZAC soldiers (from Australia and New Zealand), was a costly failure for a number of reasons. Included in these are a misjudgment of the skill and durability of the enemy and a failure to grasp the difficulty of the terrain being attacked. As a result many of the Allied troops were pinned down on the beaches and in the lower reaches of cliff faces in dreadful heat and suffering from a shortage of rations. One redeeming feature was that the eventual retreat/evacuation was carried out without significant casualties.

There were other fronts too, a number of them of little interest to those studying the role of someone in the British and Commonwealth forces, although this does not apply to sideshows in the German-held territories of Africa, in Mesopotamia, Palestine and in India.

The major battles of the war for 'Tommy' were on the Western Front and these can be difficult to unravel. Often they were not like the battles of old with defined beginnings and ends and one battle could run almost seamlessly into another. Among the very early battles of the war were Mons and the Marne; later came a number of battles around Ypres, Messines and the modern Passchendaele, Loos, Arras and later Cambrai. The summer of 1916 saw the beginning of the infamously bloody Battle of the Somme, which dragged on in various guises into 1917. The Battle of Verdun was a major attritional encounter between the French and German forces.

At sea there were major encounters in the South Atlantic early in the war followed by the massive if indecisive Battle of Jutland in 1916. Both sides also operated submarine fleets and German attempts to starve Britain by sinking any ship heading there with goods (the 'Unrestricted Submarine Warfare' of 1917), is considered the major reason for the USA joining the conflict. At first US entry merely balanced the sides, as Russia departed the war after its revolution of 1917, freeing Germany and her allies from conflict on the Eastern Front. There was also a dramatic naval raid on the Belgian port of Zeebrugge in April 1918.

As noted above (and important to a number of case studies) there was a huge spring offensive headed by German troops in March 1918 which led to many Allied casualties and prisoners of war. Then famously, on the eleventh hour of the eleventh day of the eleventh month of 1918, the guns fell silent, providing us with a very specific time when we can honour the memories of those who took part in the conflict.

I

FRED 'POP' STEPHENS:
A SAPPER'S TALE

My maternal grandfather Fred Stephens (1886–1952), known to all as 'Pop', died when I was three years old. My earliest memories are of him playing cricket and 'Cowboys and Indians' with me in a field beside his cottage in the Lake District. I remember him as a jolly, cheerful man and all that knew him back up this impression. Yet he was present at some of the events of the First World War which have since come to be regarded as the most horrific. While serving as a sapper in the Royal Engineers, he saw action in Gallipoli and later at Ypres, Messines, Passchendaele and Cambrai on the Western Front. He kept a record of his movements and thoughts throughout the war in a number of typical pocketbook diaries. By the time he returned home after the war, these were disintegrating and he transcribed them word for word into an exercise book, writing on every other side until he reached the back.

At this point, he turned the book upside-down and headed off in the opposite direction.

Fred and his two brothers (chapters two and four) were born and brought up in the iron mining and manufacturing town of Millom on the Cumbrian coast. The boys' father, Thomas, had come to the town with his own mother and stepfather.

'Pop' Stephens's transcribed diary (1919).

The family's roots were to be found around the Devon copper mines of the Tamar Valley and, before that, in the villages of the Cornish coast near Truro. The boys' mother, Jane, had come directly to Millom from a mining village close to St Austell in Cornwall. Like many God-fearing and caring miners of his day, Thomas was determined that his boys should not go underground. When he died (of anthrax) in 1907, two of the boys were settled in shop work and Fred had started behind the counter in the post office at nearby Barrow-in-Furness.

When the war broke out in 1914, Fred was a mature single man in his late twenties. He volunteered immediately but was not taken on, as his work in the post office was considered more important. His offer was finally accepted in January 1915. Clearly the war was not 'over by Christmas' 1914 as many had predicted, and more men were needed for the various campaigns being planned. He travelled to Chatham via London with a couple of post office friends – all destined to join the communications section of the Royal Engineers. (The Royal Signals had not yet been formed and many Post Office communications workers went into the Engineers, where most of the communication work was done.) All three stayed with Fred's maternal aunt, who had a small wool shop in Harlesden High Street – a stone's throw from the modern Wembley Stadium.

After arriving at Chatham the following day, and a week of 'drilling and plenty of fatigue work', Fred headed to Bulford Camp on Salisbury Plain and thence to Brookwood near Woking. Here he undertook courses in signalling, horse-riding (in some cases on mules) and musketry. The final shooting trial was held at Bisley, still famous today for its shooting competitions and currently advertising itself as 'Europe's premier shooting school'. In March 1915, his unit was inspected by George V and Queen Mary while the following weeks were spent in tents and in going through numerous war exercises.

On 20 April, his unit was inspected by the General Officer Commanding before setting out from camp: '20,000 troops, 7½ miles in length, G S wagons and everything was out for this inspection.' Five days later the first landings at Gallipoli took place but Fred was still involved in manoeuvres on the plains. In early May they were inspected once again 'for war mobilisation' but continued with 'various schemes again all over Surrey'. This continued into June with trips into local towns and the occasional catch-up with friends from back home being the only icing on the cake.

In the middle of June 1915, some of his friends left 'for the Dardanelles' and, as he put it, he 'had a good time with our mob the night before they departed – a real soldier's night out.' Fred, however, was kept back as part of the reserve and, after a few restless days, he and his unit moved to Avonmouth where they boarded the SS *Franconia*. The vessel left England on 1 July, travelled via Gibraltar and Malta, and landed at Alexandria in Egypt on 11 July. The troops from the ship moved down to Cairo for just over a week. On 20 July they boarded the tramp boat *Seang-Bee*. After three days on the ship ('food rotten and all the boys in a bad condition') they joined a flotilla off Lemnos.

On 27 July 1915, Fred saw active service for the first time as he landed on the coast of Gallipoli. At 5 a.m. he disembarked from a ship called the *Snaefell* into a barge and it took him three hours to reach the shore at Cape Helles where the original Gallipoli landing had taken place. 'Heavily shelled by the Turks on the hill – shrapnel hovering around us all the time,' he noted. By evening he and his companion signallers had reached base camp at Krithia and had dug themselves in. He covered himself with a groundsheet and when he awoke in the morning discovered that two bullets had penetrated the sheet and were lodged in the corner of the dugout. By 30 July all the 13th Division signallers were back in Lemnos via barge and ship. The first few days of active service had taken its toll; many of the men were ill and Fred described himself as 'almost a human skeleton'.

Over the next few days, Fred was to become embroiled in one of the most debated actions of the war, an action brought to the forefront by Australian film-makers in the late twentieth-century feature film *Gallipoli*. On 3 August 1915 he landed at Anzac Cove, mainly inhabited by New Zealand and Australian forces pinned down on the beach and in dugouts at the base of high cliffs. He was part of the 39th Brigade and it is clear that his job was to try to keep communications going. Just after landing, he saw his first fatality:

> Four of us went to the jetty for fresh water and had a good crack with an officer and just as we left him he got caught by a bullet and was killed. It was like Hell.

Early in August 1915, he and a party of engineers crawled up the cliffs for 1½ miles under constant fire. On their return they saw thousands of troops marching in preparation for 'a big attack on Anzac'. The aim, according to historians, was to engage the enemy while British forces landed further north at Suvla Bay in an attempt to cut off the Gallipoli peninsula. The British could then roll up and destroy the Turks in a classic pincer movement. The ANZAC attacks uphill towards the Nek and Lone Pine, with bayonets and no loaded rifles, have gone down as part of one of the most valiant and wasteful projects in warfare. Fred's description of the days surrounding these attacks is worth reproducing in full:

> Cruisers were lying outside. The 38th Brigade and Australian troops attacked the Turks at dawn and there was great shouting and heavy firing – saw quite a lot of prisoners brought in a few hours after the attack – later my officer and two of us went a mile

and a half through the gulleys and it was strewed with wounded and killed. Had a very narrow escape – snipers – managed to get a few hours' sleep on my return on the 8th – almost dead beat? Our brigade went out – heavy firing and still on top of the ridge – 39th brigade falling back. 38th brigade lost heavily on the 10th and 11th August. Some of us returned to headquarters – saw spies brought in by the Australians. On the 13th ordered again to our Brigade. It was hellish. Saw Sandy and he was a physical wreck – almost brought tears to my eyes. Will never forget the sight [*sic*] he was in.

At the time, it was believed that the bombardment from 'the cruisers' would force the Turks out of the trenches at the top of the cliffs. This was not the case and a combination of confusion over timing and shattered communication wires meant that those ascending the cliffs were met by a fully prepared opposition. This led to the carnage described in the diary, the film and history books.

With little achieved in terms of progress, it was a case of stalemate with troops unable to move inland from Anzac Cove or Suvla Bay. More than three weeks after the attack at Anzac, Fred was transferred to the Bay exhausted 'for want of sleep and rest'. At this point in the diary and with no explanation he wrote, 'the S.M. was a *coward*'. On 6 September, he noted, 'first night's sleep and rest since 12 August'.

The campaign was now in limbo and during this period he was given his first new shirt since leaving home and also received a food parcel from Millom. By the middle of October most of the Allied soldiers still had two or three months left before total withdrawal. Not so for Fred:

While at Suvla Bay, an abscess formed on my face, unable to stop the discharge and saw the Dr on the 18th October. Quite a number of our signallers ill owing to the heat and quite a number of them were sent to Hospital. 29th October – very heavy shelling and saw 2 killed and 14 wounded right in front of us – 'twas an awful sight. Face still discharging a lot and was ordered to Hospital – feeling O.K. and fit in myself. Got on board hospital ship Letitia on 7 November at Suvla Bay and reached Lemnos 9th.

From Lemnos he was moved to Malta and the hospital at St Andrew's Barracks. The doctors wanted to remove a tooth but Fred insisted on having them all removed. He was sent home on the SS *Kildonian Castle* and by 29 November he was in Netley Hospital, having all his bottom teeth removed. After a week, he was allowed home on leave. Ten days later he was summoned to the signals department at Bletchley where he met a few Post Office friends including Sandy Bayne. The next few months were spent here in billets at Newport Pagnell and with occasional trips home.

In March 1916, Fred was promoted to lance corporal (unpaid) and, before leaving for France 'in charge of a party', met up with Sandy who was off to Mesopotamia. Fred's unit landed at Le Havre then transferred to Abbeville. From here he went 'on draft' to the 2nd Army at Cassel where he spent almost three months on 'a course of wireless work and amplifier'.

The diary entry for 30 June 1916 proved one of the most dramatic:

Myself and interpreter (from Scotch [*sic*] Regiment) for Armentières on amplifying work. In trenches only a few yards from the front line (slept in half Moon shaped dug out). It was here that Fritz came over one night and was driven back but my pal and I heard nothing, although we did hear a few stray bullets whizzing around and often hit our dugout. When we opened the barricaded door in the early hours of the morning, we saw a Tommy on sentry duty and he was greatly surprised to see us there, told us we were very lucky fellows.

After a fortnight in the front line, he returned to Armentières and from there went to join the 5th Corps at Dranoutre. In early August 1916, he moved to Wulgerham where he became involved in moves to undermine the German lines:

> Lots of sniping going on – went about 2 miles down the mines – underground – made by the engineers – towards Messines with amplifier – heard the Germans working with pick and shovel and heard conversations which were very faint. Not a pleasant job having to creep a good distance and up to knees in mud and water in some places.

Over the next few months he was back and forwards from the front line until 7 April 1917 when he went to visit a friend in a billet in Bailleul. Half an hour after he left, 'Fritz dropped a bomb and seriously injured him. Died on the 9th.'

In early June he was moved gradually up towards Messines Ridge and was only a mile away from the ridge on 5 June when it was blown up. At the end of July he was in the trenches and hunting for his brother John but with 'no luck', as his brother had left a few hours before his arrival. In August 1917 he was sent to the 107th Brigade and 'had a narrow squeak' finding his way to headquarters. On 14 August while at C Bank Ypres, he had another hair-raising experience:

> Wandered to battalion headquarters thro treacherous country and muddy – it was wicked – on one occasion had to take cover behind a tank which had been put out of action – it was wicked having to carry full round of ammunition, rifles and w/t set. Fixed out a set in one of Jerry's concrete dugouts. About 3 a.m. I went out and laid out 4 lines – one of which I had to crawl almost within a few yards of the enemy's line. About 4 a.m. heavy firing and artillery commenced and no signals could be heard.

Went out again under heavy firing and repaired all the lines and it was useless trying to repair them a third time – smashed to atoms. Captain Redmond was brought in wounded and had orders to pack up as the enemy was advancing and would soon be on us. My officer was the first to go and we toddled on with all our pack and w/t set. Shells dropping all around us. My pal was just behind us until a certain point but when headquarters was reached, he was missing. After a rest, I volunteered to go back and search for him but the o.c [*sic*] said it was too risky – apparently he was killed by a stray bullet or shrapnel. My name was taken by the o/c and later we were told that the l/c got a military medal. It was a proper death trap and lucky to come out alive.

The entries from August to November 1917 are rather thin. He moved around France and Belgium a great deal, had some leave and spent some time fruitlessly searching for his brother. In mid-November he moved from Ypres to Haveringcourt where the headquarters of the Cambrai sector lay. On 20 November he watched the first massed tank advance in history:

Big attack at 9 a.m. – from our position which would be 1½ miles from the attack we could see the tanks in operation driving the Germans out of the wood and Canal Bank. It was a wonderful sight. About 8 or a dozen tanks in a line. At dusk I went out with my officer and 2 more chaps – full pack and set – thro Hindenburg Line – thick with barbed wire and very deep trenches. Found we were in No Man's Land – flare lights going up by the enemy and we were absolutely lost; so our o/i/c gave order to return to Headquarters at 9 p.m. It was an awful experience finding our way back. By the time we reached Headqrs we were absolutely dead beat. Our great coats, breeches and puttees were ripped with barbed wire entanglement. Big ration of rum given us at Hdqrs and slept like a top after it in our sodden clothes.

He remained at Headquarters until the middle of December when he was struck down by appendicitis. From here he was transported back to England via Boulogne. After an operation in Manchester and recuperation, he went on a wireless course. From here he went to the Signal Department in Bedford where he played cricket and was involved in varied 'signal work'. He moved from here to Catterick where he was when the armistice was signed in November. He was eventually discharged on 31 January 1919.

THE TALE BEHIND THE TALE

The transcribed diary and other wartime souvenirs were left to my father who had also served as a signaller in the Royal Signals in the Second World War. When I was young, my father would not let me see the diary, saying that my grandfather had said it was too personal for me to look at. Later my father confided that he alone had been the censor, worried that I would be upset by the contents. From what I could remember of my grandfather, I felt that he would have wanted me and youngsters in particular to know about his experiences. I was thus pleased to research them in detail and to share my findings with others while serving as a secondary school teacher.

My grandfather left a number of interesting war souvenirs but the diary was the most useful and informative, alongside a couple of newspaper extracts he had glued inside the front and back covers. One of these extracts has proved to be an exceptionally interesting and educational piece of evidence. This is a cutting from the local newspaper containing a letter Fred had written home to his mother while en route for Gallipoli. In describing the journey from Avonmouth to Malta, he wrote:

Card-playing, sleeping and singing are the chief doings with mouth organs and melodeons; it generally starts about 7 p.m. and the boys go at it full steam until about 9.30; it is a treat! You talk about the Barrow to Fleetwood trips – they are nothing compared to this. There are about _____ [excision by censor] of us on board and a lively lot too. Get to bed about ten o clock. The food is tip top and we dine second class saloon!! So far on our journey have seen two ships each day on the horizon – no doubt mail or passenger boats. Could do with about three months of this – a trip to Canada or Australia would suit me down to the ground.

The aim of the letter is clearly to put his mother at ease; the Barrow to Fleetwood trip was a well-known local 'lads' day out. By contrast, in his diary for the same period, he refers to being abandoned by the escorting destroyers, followed by enemy submarines and 'having a rough passage over the Bay of Biscay'. The famous writer Compton McKenzie had experienced accommodation on the *Franconia* a few weeks earlier. He was having lunch on board with a group of medics:

I happened to ask why we had been given second-class cabins.

'I'll show you why after lunch,' said one of them.

Getting hold of a key from the steward, he took me along and opened the door to what looked like a Bluebeard's Chamber. From floor to ceiling the white cabin was splashed with blood.

'We brought back 5,000 wounded in this ship and they haven't had time to clear up the relics.'

Fred hadn't really told lies in his letter home; he had just neglected to tell the whole truth. This is a useful call to caution for researchers when using primary evidence like this.

The other newspaper extract contains the obituary of Sandy Bayne, Fred's friend and, reading between the lines, possibly his best friend. Sandy's name crops up a number of times in Fred's diary, particularly on one occasion when they came across each other in Gallipoli and burst into tears when they saw the shape they were both in. The wonders of the modern search engine reveal the following information on the Barrow-in-Furness war memorial site:

BAYNE, William George. Sergeant, 62357, Army Signal Company, Royal Engineers. Died of disease on 25th July 1916. Buried in Basra War Cemetery.

The faded obituary, headed by a photograph and the strap line 'Died in Persian Gulf', revealed a career almost parallel to that of Fred Stephens (although Sandy was five years older). He was a sergeant at the time of his death, promoted after spending a massive fifty-seven hours at his signalling post in Gallipoli. He was captain of the GPO football team for which Fred played and left a wife and two children. This is a sad story magnified thousands of times between 1914 and 1918. In learning about war, youngsters in particular are often overawed and uncom-prehending when the sheer number of casualties is given them. Learning of the loss of a single much cherished individual can be equally effective in getting across the message of the tragedy of war.

Fred's diary also contains dark asides. On 16 November 1916, he reported 'slightly gassed – not to be forgotten'. This weak-ened his heart and may have been responsible for his death in 1952, weeks after his retirement from the post office. There were lighter sides too. At one point, he was sitting in a French village cafe when the East Lancs Regiment passed by. Recognising a couple of Millom lads, he leapt up and gave them each a cold beer on what was a very warm July day. Soon after he went to headquarters for rations and recorded 'blotto one night and all rations went in a ditch and got soaked'. Early in 1917 he attended a concert in the sergeants' mess – 'lost bikes in the middle of the road – 'nuff said', he wrote. Such releases from the horrors of the front line were essential even for those who were fairly sober in nature back in 'Civvy Street'.

'Pop' Stephens's map with circles around places visited.

Research Tip: Compare and Contrast

It is wise to test any personal family primary sources against wider histories of the same event or events, both primary and secondary based. An online history of the 13th Division, for example, came up with the following in connection with activity from February to August 1915:

Towards the end of February the entire Division concentrated at Blackdown in Hampshire.

On 7 June 1915, orders were received to prepare to move to the Mediterranean. All mechanical transport was withdrawn and the first reinforcement drafts were ordered not to sail (other than those for the artillery).

Entire Division landed at ANZAC Cove between 3–5 August 1915.

All these statements fit with the account of his movements as given by Fred Stephens in his diary. This increases the value of both the diary and the divisional history as historical sources.

Other memorabilia left by Fred serves to add to our knowledge of life for a Tommy on active service. These include the handle of a German officer's dress sword (now on a plinth in my study), a scarf of Belgian lace bought for his mother, a huge woven tapestry showing the Allied flags with a space in the middle for a photograph, a bullet casing and a small collection of photo cards showing Ypres after the conflict. Most useful of all is a map of the Western Front upon which he has marked all the places he visited during the war.

The tale behind Fred's tale ends with a couple of musings. Many of my books and articles urge researchers to ask questions of elderly relatives as soon as possible. I never had the opportunity to do this with my grandfather. I would ask him why he wrote his single stark comment on the seargeant major's cowardice and also why he and his friends hid in the coal bunker of the hospital ship when it made its first stop on the way from Gallipoli. Had he had enough and feared being patched up and sent straight back? Now we will never know.

The final musing refers to the irony of Fred's circumstances. For centuries the Stephens family had crawled around in tunnels underground digging out metal ore (I still have Thomas Stephens's Victorian working pick in my study). Thomas was determined that his boys would not go down the mine. For a short time at least, Fred spent his life crawling around in an underground mine up to his knees in mud and water in conditions far worse than those experienced at Millom's Hodbarrow iron ore mine. These conditions were exposed in full in the recent Australian feature film *Under Hill 60* – a war film worth watching if there was any family involvement in the Messines campaign.

2

JOHN STEPHENS:
A PRISONER OF WAR'S TALE

Fred Stephens (chapter one) was the second of three brothers. His elder brother, John, was working in the furniture section of the Co-operative Wholesale Society in Liverpool when war broke out in August 1914. In November of the same year, he married Millicent (Lily) Swindale – a girl from back home in Millom. He enlisted in the King's (Liverpool) Regiment in November 1915 but was not mobilised until March 1917 as private No. 203228 in the KLR's 12th Battalion.

John began service on the Western Front in late 1917 as part of a Lewis gun crew and was unfortunate enough to be just to the south west of St Quentin when the Germans began their determined if ultimately unsuccessful 'final push' on the Western Front in March 1918. On 24 March he was taken prisoner. Between the time of his capture and his return to the family's home base in Cumberland at the end of November 1918, he kept a detailed account of all that happened to him. The tale that follows is based wholly on extracts from that account:

23 March 1918
Dug trench for Lewis gun. Officer had wind up, produced his revolver to show us he wasn't nervous. HA HA. Didn't see him any more. Jerry got very lively toward evening – we escaped damage. Troops up above suffered heavily. 8 of us found m gun man wounded so took him to Ham. Passed through several villages, all troops gone and aid posts. Borrowed (?) ladder to carry man, finished up with a stretcher on a wooden barrow. Very long journey, poor chap in a mess.

24 March 1918
Gun posts outside Ham. 4 of us slept in empty house until 6 am. Left at 6.40. Jerry in the vicinity so hooked it. Walked north for some miles but found Jerry ahead of us. 5 of us captured 8.30. 3 Jerrys to each man – all provided with revolvers. One asked me if I was a gentleman. Naturally I said yes. My captors let me keep my knife and haversack. Other fellows lost theirs. Just after capture, Jerry's army attacked by three planes – hot stuff also heavy mc fire from Jerry. We stayed by wagon and escaped any damages – ordered by Jerry officer to walk back alone. Walked all day past thousands of troops, foot, cavalry, guns, pontoons etc. Jerry very good so far – always gave us water first before having their share. Officer gave us drink from his flask. Lots of troops could speak English fluently. Saw lots of our dead lying around. Exchanged my putties for three cigars, finished up my biscuits, first feed for the day.

Soon after capture, the men of the 12th KLR were placed together with other prisoners. For the following few weeks they were kept locally, put to work firstly on a railway then on a canal. They survived mainly on barley soup and water:

10 May 1918

Up 5.30. Extra fine morning – work on the new railway – a good time. Dinner at 3 – boiled fruit – jam for tea – still 6 to a loaf. Saw aeroplane brought down in flames. Saw Jerry's observation sausage brought down – daren't show delight – some of Jerrys vexed.

Little changed during May although the quality of both food and drink gradually started to improve. By early June, they were still near Ham and billeted in a chateau. The big change came in the middle of June. After three months of captivity, the prisoners were gathered together in a large group and 'entrained in trucks' for Germany. The journey took a couple of days and John noted that they passed through Strasbourg and Colmar:

15 June 1918

Up at 4 a.m. – soup and twelve to a loaf – rations cut down owing to fellows stealing bread. Entrained in trucks (covered) at 7.30 for Germany travelling two days. Plenty of straw to lie on. Excellent meals on the journey – best since captured – meat, fruit, barley, bread and macaroni at different stops on the journey. Prisoners help themselves with coffee – great idea. Feeding arrangements splendid for long journey.

Within a few days John was settled in a camp close to Freiburg and the Rhine and seemed relatively happy for the first time, noting the following in his diary:

18 June 1918

Lovely country, loads of fruit on the roadside ... Reveille at 4.30. Huts and beds to clean by 6.30. Bkfast at 7 of soup, extra good and buckshee. Walked to neighbouring town for bath and fumigation. Crossed the Rhine. Straw beds provided during afternoon. For the first time since capture felt clean. Slept without trousers. Lovely country, loads of fruit on the roadside.

Things then took a turn for the worse. His legs began to swell and he was placed in a civilian hospital for some considerable time. He was not the only prisoner to suffer:

27 June 1918

Deaths average two or three a day for this week.

By early July, his health had begun to improve and he started to help around the hospital – mostly by dressing wounds and peeling potatoes. Then stomach problems set in and he wrote:

6 July 1918

Sim from camp didn't know me. Thin, eyes sunk back and ½ inch beard. Had the wind up when I saw myself in a glass. Didn't expect to get better.

This ill health continued until the middle of July when he returned to the main camp and began to teach himself shorthand. Soon he was on light duties and in early August became part of a work detail taken into the local town:

? August 1918

Glorious morning. Up at 5.30. Went with eight fellows and one guard to Freiburg for blankets. Grand ride in train. Spoke to Jerry who had been at Gun Farm (Whyschette). Freiburg lovely town, splendid countryside, large palm trees. Soldiers gave me bread, cigarettes and barley soup. Bread from a nun. Whilst sitting on the stairs in a café, German waitress said 'Ullo, Tommy'. She had been to Liverpool, London and USA. Quite homely. Arrived back at 8.30. Civi gave me apple. Spoke to a fellow at the station – idea one of our spies.

By the middle of August he had been put to work at unloading iron beams. The work was hard but, by now, John was sensing that things were not going well for his captors:

25 August 1918
Noticed Jerry engineers clothes made of paper.

About this time he was given a job working in a photographic shop where the Germans were taking pictures of men about to go up the line. He was rarely short of food now but the sounds of war were getting increasingly closer. By September he had an inkling that the war was turning against the Germans:

3 September 1918
Rumours of USA advance. Jerry's observation balloon seen in the distance.

Now adept at scrounging cigarettes, cigars and extra food, he was moved from the photographic shop and ordered to clear the ground for a landing strip for German planes.

By the middle of September, food had started to be rationed and his greatcoat had been stolen – by a German he suspected. Incarceration was also taking its toll:

A mirror made by John from glass and part of an airplane wing.

23 September 1918
Weighed on scale at dump. 8 stone all on. Must have been 7st in hospital. Terrible

By October he was involved in maize and potato production, and making do and mend as far as food was concerned. Talk of a peace conference was also rife:

14 October 1918
Rumours again. Jerry says rumours true

And there was still time for mischief:

17 October 1918
During one of the baths trips one of the fellows managed to get on the side of the road with the apple trees. I did once and had a good whack from Jerry for getting apples. Ginger [a guard?] trounced me and made me, or thought he did, give up all I had – but worked on farm digging a trench for vegetables and more spuds in my pocket.

Also:

19 October 1918
Boiled spuds at 10.30. Roast ditto at 1. Packed some beauties inside my shirt – or all that is left of one – also coat pockets. When we arrived back at farm, Jerry sergt had us searched – result exit potatoes.

By late October, confusion reigned. The prisoners were moved out into billets near Saarbrücken and virtually abandoned. They went out in parties to scrounge for food and became increasingly reliant on the generosity of the civilian population. John was billeted in a glassworks when he wrote the following entry on a day forever etched in world history:

11 November 1918

Up at 6.30. Misty. Coffee and bread and jam at 7. Can see into the town from our window. Rumours of Kaiser and C Prince giving up throne to the socialists. Orders to take it quietly before moving again. Jerry officer came up to tell war finished. English, French and German evac. Hurrah! Lovely day like summer. Gloomy thoughts about home. Rumours about Old Bill and family in Holland. Gave word of honour to officer not to attempt to run away. Sent us with guards without rifles – first time since prisoner for a good walk through town and out into the country through a big wood – any amount of stumps – Christmas trees growing a treat. Jerry guards short of wind and same Tommy. Lamps were lighted in the town tonight.

And on the first days of 'peace' that followed:

12 November 1918

Up at 6.15. WC twice. Nice morning. Four to loaf. Sudden orders to move at 12. Train (2nd class) to Fosbach and joined other prisoners bound for home. Most of these chaps had had their parcels and took pity on us. Two boys gave Lovell and I such a feed of fish, flesh, biscuits and real butter – fit for a king – full for the first time in five weeks – nearly bust. Too full to sleep – stayed one night in a large hall and cleaned officers' boots.

13 November 1918

Up at 5.30. Officer in command told us we could wait about 14 days for a train if we liked or walk to French lines in four or five days. Decided on the latter. Started at 7.30 – walked to St Avola nineteen kilos and stayed the night. Saw a long train of Jerry soldiers decorated with red flags – they gave us a cheer. Our guards dumped their rifles and pack on a cart – some got drunk. Supposed to march four deep did that for about fifty yards then strolled as we liked with our bundle of rags. Lavelle and I drummed up rest of spuds and flesh. Had a good sleep. Stayed in large stables – sort of racing establishment. Was called in the house by a civi and given fried potatoes – no need for peelings now. Heel and toe getting sore. Boys enjoyed big campfire of shavings etc before turning in.

By 16 November he had limped south-westwards to Nancy and into American hands. His feet were so badly swollen that he had to wear a size nine boot on one foot and a size seven on the other. The Americans insisted that he wait for an ambulance train. On 19 November, he reached Calais where he remained until crossing the Channel on the afternoon of 24 November. After being medically discharged as B3 at Dover, he began the last leg of his journey:

27 November 1918
Parade for train about 10. Broke journey at Willesden Jnct. Gave Gran and all a fright. First news of Lil and mother for over 8 months.

28 November 1918
Caught mid-day train W Junct for Millom. Arrived at Millom during the evening. Lil surprised me at Green Road. Great welcome.

Once home, he was still officially 'on leave'. During this time he relied to a great extent on his 'Repatriated Prisoner of War's Leave or Duty Ration book' which contained stamps for cheese, jam, tea, meat and lard. Many of the stamps have been used. On 18 March 1919, he returned his greatcoat and on 8 April 1919 was transferred to the reserve and signed off at Preston. For the following twelve months he received a pension of 15s a week. This came to an end on 6 April 1920.

THE TALE BEHIND THE TALE

In 1919, a booklet was produced in Liverpool analysing what had happened to the men from the King's (Liverpool) Regiment who had become prisoners of war. An extract from this reads:

> The German Spring Offensive of March and April 1918 resulted in the capture of an additional number of over 1,100 men belonging to the 4th, 5th, 7th, 11th, 12th and 13th battalions … In time, but in many cases not for several weeks, they were registered at Prison Camps in Germany but were themselves made to perform heavy manual labour on food which was not more than enough to maintain existence

For more on this see chapter three.

This account fits in admirably with John's experiences. For the first three months of captivity he was used on manual labour near to the front lines as the Germans kept up hopes of further advances. By the time he was sent to a camp in Germany, the German war effort had begun to unravel and what organisation there was gradually melted away leaving the prisoners to fend for themselves.

In light of what happened to John, it is possible to extract a number of themes from his writings.

It is said of human beings that their first concerns are for food, clothing and shelter. Reference to numerous accounts of life on active service generally teaches that 'shelter' was the least important of the three – soldiers who were tired learned to sleep anywhere. In the case of a prisoner of war, a third pertinent theme might therefore be general treatment at the hands of the captors.

Food

Given the choice between food and clothing, food clearly comes first. In the diary hardly a day passes without reference to the search for food. Bread was a vital commodity and daily satisfaction was based on the number of prisoners to a loaf. The average was three to five prisoners to a loaf while six or above was cause for complaint. A single loaf all to himself was noted with joy. Later in captivity, the potato became a vital commodity.

Research Tip: Oh for a Smoke!

Look out for references to smoking! While late twentieth-century research on the damage done by smoking has put a considerable damper on the activity, the First World War was a golden age for the cigarette. 'Smile' when you had a 'lucifer to light your fag' was the suggestion of a popular song of the day. Fred 'Pop' Stephens (chapter one) certainly enjoyed his cigarettes and was pleased when he was given some 'fags' as a prize for doing well in a cross-country run. Such a reward would be unthinkable today. In his POW diary, Fred's brother John (chapter two) judged the success of his day not only by the food secured but by the smokes he managed to scrounge. Most of these were acquired from German soldiers or members of the public and a complete cigar was considered to be a real treat. On a wider theme, perhaps the best loved padre of the war was known as 'Woodbine Willie', as he always seemed to have a soothing selection of that particular brand of cigarettes for those he met. The term 'tab' also came into common use as wartime economies necessitated the production of smaller 'tab' cigarettes.

The first three months of captivity were the worst when it came to food and drink. On occasions during this period, they sometimes had nothing before midday and that at a time when they were involved in hard manual labour. A month after his captivity John noted 'nothing for 26 hours'. Black bread and barley were often the staple diet, though in the first few weeks in Germany the food situation improved and there was meat, honey and thick broth. Tea and coffee seemed to be readily available too. As the German war effort began to wane, provisions became poor again and he noted on 14 September that the food was 'as bad as the first three months a prisoner'. In these circumstances his fellow prisoners were known to resort to snails on toast. From here onwards there are numerous references to scavenging parties going out in search of food.

Clothing

The references to clothing are rarer. For the first few weeks the POWs worked and slept in the clothes in which they had been captured and it was a long time before John had a wash or a bath. Later he refers to being given a form of prison uniform and mentions mending and washing his shirt from time to time. The loss of his greatcoat caused him considerable anguish although it seems that he was provided with another one weeks later. One of the most interesting references in this context is to a German soldier wearing paper clothing near the end of the war.

Treatment

John's arrival home 'medically B3' indicates that his general treatment had been poor. This was not the cruelty and inhumanity of some infamous camps of the Second World War yet, as the post-war analysis suggests, being put to strenuous labour on meagre rations could only have one outcome. The food situation has already been discussed. For the first three months the prisoners were forced into jobs which would aid the German advance: building a railway, working on a canal and moving ammunition around close to the battlefront. On one occasion John spent a few nights in an old YMCA hut, a sign that the enemy was still advancing through the Allied lines. When in Germany he spent the latter part of the war constructing an aerodrome and unpacking planes. Just prior to this he had worked in a photographic shop, preparing official pictures of German soldiers, a job he described as both 'indoors' and 'A1'. The topic of using POWs for war work is one often debated; the only possible plus side was that he was 'paid' for it – 3s a week – and that he used this money from time-to-time to purchase certain creature comforts.

The lesson of history is that wars, revolutions and civil wars bring out both the best and worst in people and John's treatment as a POW backs this up. In general the civilian population was helpful and friendly, even in Germany. Many locals went out of their way to talk to him and other prisoners and to provide them from time-to-time with food, drink, cigars and cigarettes. This was not always the case with the soldiers who were looking after him. One particular guard he called 'Ginger' or 'the old devil' was described on more than one occasion as a 'pig'. He was not averse to kicking and striking prisoners and threatening to shoot those who did not work hard. At the same time there are numerous references to friendly German soldiers, often those who had served in the same area of the front as John. Many of them could speak English and John was particularly fulsome in praise of an officer he met just prior to the end of the war – he had lived in Coventry for some time prior to 1914 and was 'a real gentleman'. John was also able to take solace from reading. A devoted Methodist and choirmaster, he obtained a Bible while in Germany and read it daily. He also read fiction books including one by Rider Haggard, author of *King Solomon's Mines*.

As was the case in other prison camps, prisoners did not get along among themselves all the time. While in Germany, there was one prisoner whom John referred to as 'the bully'. He smacked John once as he was warming up his coffee on a stove. The same bully was taught a lesson later by a Welsh soldier and John noted that his attacker was 'hammered' and that his face was 'all different colours' afterwards.

Only a single swift reading of the entire diary really gives an overview of John's circumstances. He did not have a wash for the first three weeks of his captivity or a bath for the first six weeks. He was massively underweight most of the time and suffered from stomach problems constantly. He spent some considerable time in hospital and off duties as a result of this, and also due to problems with his legs. Many of his companions died or spent even longer spells in hospital. When in hospital himself in June, he heard the German orderly saying 'Englander kaput' a number of times in his ward and noted himself that he and his friend Gibbs 'were slowly passing away'. His daughter Joan said that it took him a long time to recuperate after the war.

On further reflection perhaps the saddest entry in his diaries was one made on 11 November 1918, the very last day of the war. It reads simply – 'gloomy thoughts of home'. Why gloomy, one might ask? This was in all probability because he had left behind a wife, a mother who would now be sixty and a maternal grandmother who would be in her early eighties. He had not heard of any of them for nine months and could not be certain that they would still be alive when he reached England. And John's story does not finish here. It continues in the next case study where material has survived which allows us to examine the wartime experiences of his nearest and dearest back home.

3

LIL STEPHENS: TALE OF A POW'S WIFE

il (Millicent Mary) Swindale married John Stephens soon after the outbreak of war. She was over thirty and belonged to a metal mining family that had moved into Millom from the lead mines of the Northern Pennines and the copper mines of the Lake District in the late nineteenth century. Her marriage meant a transfer to Liverpool and when John joined the army she took up a position in the post office there. Once she was told that John was 'missing believed killed' she moved back to Millom to live with her mother-in-law. She was here when John returned from captivity in November 1918.

Although there is no sign of a diary for Lil during this period, much of the paperwork built up in the search for her missing husband has survived and this allows us to build up a picture of her activity back home. Uncertain for most of the time whether he was dead or alive, she made every effort to find out what she could about him and, once he was known to be alive and a POW, she did her best to help him out where possible. By putting her efforts alongside matching information from John's diary, we can reconstruct scenes which must have been repeated in many British homes around this time, although many did not enjoy the same happy outcome.

Lil's tale starts soon after John 'went missing' on 24 March 1918. Shortly after this date, she began to receive pieces of formal notification from the War Office. One was in the form of a narrow slip of paper stating that 'Missing' did not necessarily mean that the soldier was 'killed or wounded'. This was accompanied by a two-sided document entitled 'Missing Officers and Men', which set out details of the efforts to find him that would be made by his Commanding Officer, the British Red Cross and the Order of St John. The same document also referred to attempts being made to find him in enemy territory through the good offices of the neutral Dutch government. A third document (undated) was headed 'Notice to Wives and other Dependents of Soldiers reported missing'. This covered the separation allowance already being paid out and noted that the allowance would come to an end thirty weeks after John had been reported missing. It would then be replaced by a pension yet, at the same time, 'it was not to be taken that the soldier was dead'. Ultimately any final settlements and arrangements would be made by the Army Council when it was 'able to accept the soldier as dead for official purposes'. The pensioner would be informed 'when this has been done'. John's return home alive seems to have coincided more or less with this thirty week cut-off point.

The first date discernible for action by Lil herself is 14 May 1918 and is in the form of a letter sent to the Red Cross in Switzerland containing John's details. In return she received a standard letter dated 3 June that acknowledged receipt of her correspondence and stated that the best would be done to make all possible enquiries and that she would be kept informed. This letter was from the 'Enquiry Department for Wounded and Missing' of the British Red Cross and Order of St John. A further communication then arrived from the Queen Victoria Jubilee Fund Association in Geneva dated 20 June. This was also in response to Lil's letter of 14 May and informed her that John's details were to be placed on the next circular (No. 49) to be distributed around camps and hospitals in Germany. His name was still on Circular No. 50 in August 1918, which is among the family papers. His entry here states simply: 'Private J Stephens 203228 A Co King's Liverpool Rifles, missing March 21st 1918.'

The August entry, around five months after his captivity, is interesting for a number of reasons. It indicates that none of the surviving witnesses had seen him for at least three days before his capture, which is recorded as 24 March in his diary. Also it would seem that his name remained on the 'missing' list after there was proof that he was still alive.

At some point in June (and probably later rather than earlier), Lil, now in Millom, received a card with three stamps on it –

An official card from John stating that he is a POW.

one discernible as 3 June and postmarked Geneva. It had been delivered initially to her address in Liverpool and was an official German War Department postcard. On the back, it states: 'Fill up this card immediately' and 'I am prisoner of war in Germany'. John appears to have followed the first instruction. He had merely added his name and the fact that he was 'sound'. The date of writing was 16 April – three weeks after his capture. About seven weeks later it was posted from Geneva and it was a further two weeks or more before it reached his wife.

Once Lil knew that her husband was alive and a prisoner, she contacted the local voluntary war service bureau in Liverpool. This bureau had been set up to look after prisoners in the KLR. A lengthy missive from the bureau dated 1 July 1918 thanks her for her letter of 26 June and for giving 'the latest address' for her husband. It also tells her what she needs to do in order to get a parcel of extra comforts to him. There were also details of what

A list of possible parcel 'goodies' sent to Lil by the Liverpool Committee.

could be placed in the parcel at her chosen cost of 4s a week. A card from the same office dated 7 October noted that her funds had run out and she needs to continue a payment of £1 every five weeks (which is effectively 4s a week).

On 25 November, and now back in England, John filled in the standard War Office 'I am safe card'. It read:

Prisoners of War Reception Camp at Dover – I have been released and expect to be home shortly Letter follows at first opportunity – signed John.

The date apart, all was a typed template except for 'Dover' and 'John', which were in his own handwriting. He had also crossed out sections referring to the possibility of his being 'wounded', 'sick' or 'in hospital'. He posted it to his home address in Liverpool from where it was forwarded to his wife in Millom. It probably landed on the doormat after he had wiped his feet there. Letters from John to his wife from the various camps have also survived. The notepaper on which the letters were written is undated and the envelopes are fixed with stamps dating mostly for late November 1918, again after he had returned home.

THE TALE BEHIND THE TALE

Lil's tale has been told chronologically. If the story then seems a little mechanical, the approach does allow the yale behind the tale to take a more emotive look at what was going on 'behind the scenes'. As with John's study (chapter two), the 1919 LWWSB (Liverpool Women's War Service Bureau) post-war analysis of what happened to KLR prisoners of war is helpful. According to the report, the Spring Offensive of 1918 led to the capture of over 1,000 men from the regiment and brought 'the number of prisoners under the care of the bureau to a total of 2,244'. This meant a staggering doubling of captives to be sought out over a matter of days. The author of the same review adds:

A very large number of these men were allowed by the German authorities to inform their relatives that they were prisoners, but were not allowed to give any address to which parcels or correspondence might be sent.

After noting that many were kept behind the lines for several weeks and put to work before being sent to Germany, the report continues:

So much has been published in the press concerning the condition of the men captured during this period that it is not necessary to enlarge upon the subject, but the contrast between those men working behind the lines with those who had been receiving regular supplies of parcels and those whose parcels had not reached them has been most marked.

In this respect John was one of the unlucky ones. From all the paperwork on both sides of the Channel, it is clear that he received no parcels and no correspondence at any time during his captivity. Before family knowledge of his survival and possible whereabouts, this is understandable. What is distressing is that the later efforts to help him were unsuccessful despite the time and money dedicated to these efforts. The topic of correspondence raises its head often in John's diaries. He writes cards and letters to his wife and mother on a regular basis. He was unaware that they were destined to spend a long time in the post with the majority of them arriving just in time for him to read them out personally. He also expresses the desire to receive letters from home and, in particular, food parcels. This desire becomes stronger the longer he is held captive and, towards the end, he refers constantly to rumours that parcels were on the way, at one point suggesting that they were to be picked up from a local town 'within the week'. In reality, the only food parcel he encountered belonged to another prisoner he met and that was devoured two days after the armistice. The result of this encounter was, in his own words, that he was 'fit to bust'.

Again, returning to all the paperwork connected to John's captivity, it is clear that nobody in England knew exactly where he was being kept prisoner at any one time. The likelihood of any parcel reaching him must therefore have been low, especially when in Germany the native population and armed forces were in decline and facing starvation themselves.

For those researching ancestral POWs during this period, Lil and John's tale provides some helpful guidelines to material likely to be useful in reconstructing their stories. This includes official documentation from the War Office, written links to the Red Cross and, in particular, any written material relating to a local or regional war service bureau set up to find and support the prisoners. The post-war report issued by the Liverpool Committee proved extremely helpful in putting John's experiences in context. The wartime material dealing with parcels was also most informative although, ironically, of little practical help to the prisoner in this case. At one point Lil was told that she could, as 'adopter' (the term used for one who paid to support a POW), provide for three parcels of foodstuff per fortnight and 13lb of bread. On a quarterly basis, the bureau could also forward a parcel with 'extra comforts such as Shaving Outfit, Cleaning Materials, Toilet Necessaries, Cap Badge, etc. etc.' In this case the next of kin needed to apply to the Board for a personal Parcel Coupon. A complete set of clothing was sent every six months but this was 'supplied officially – no subscriptions required for this purpose'. After the German Spring Offensive, the annual cost to the bureau of 'men under their care' rose from £21,000 to £75,000.

Joan, John's daughter, wrote to me on the subject of the correspondence covering chapters two and three. She observed that 'very few of his letters reached them and none of theirs reached him in the prison camp'. In this context it is interesting and important to look at all the correspondence that has survived and, in particular, the date stamps on the envelopes. John informed the authorities that he was safe in April. Those at home were given this information in June. He, on the other hand, remained totally in the dark about his family back home, even addressing his last correspondence from Dover to his Liverpool home when his wife had been in Millom for nine months. He clearly missed her while a prisoner. Joan said that the letters that did arrive were too personal to publish and in one of the better days in his diary he ended by saying 'all that was missing was Lil'.

This tale does, however, have a happy ending. A welcoming party awaited him at Millom station but Lil got onto the train a couple of stops before so their own reunion could be as personal as possible. From Millom to Merseyside and from St Quentin to Strasbourg, the story of John and Lil must have been mirrored thousands of times. The joy here is that enough material has survived for me to be able to retell that tale almost a century later.

4

CHARLES STEPHENS
(1888–1972): TALE FROM A
'FORGOTTEN FRONT'

Charlie was the youngest of the three Stephens brothers (chapters one to three). When war broke out, like his oldest brother, he was already married to a local girl. Like John he too was working in the Co-operative but in his case close to home in the small village of Haverigg near Millom. He was called up in January 1917 and linked up with the Royal Field Artillery at Preston. He remained in training on the Lancashire coast until April 1917 when he moved south to Bulford Camp and trained as a signaller. On 28 September 1917, he boarded the *Balmoral Castle*, a troopship bound for India. The journey to India took two months and followed the long route round the horn of Africa.

Like his elder brothers, Charlie was a diarist; in fact his diaries were the most detailed of the three which, in some respects, is a shame as his service, though strictly speaking 'active', was not destined to be 'in the thick of it'. At the same time, lack of such activity serves to explain why he had the time to write in detail.

The sea journey was not without incident. Charlie found himself a little sideline serving in the sergeants' mess and received payment for his work which came in handy when he reached his destination. As was general practice on these lengthy journeys, there was a short stopover at Durban where the men were allowed ashore. After the break, they were placed on a new ship – the RMS *Caronia*. Although larger, this was a slightly older vessel and for some reason or another, more cramped. (Possibly troops from more than one vessel had now been placed on board as was common practice.) Charlie reported on restlessness among the men and sentries on board with fixed bayonets during the remaining fortnight of the trip.

On landing there was a two-day trip from Mumbai to the base camp at Mhow where Charlie began duties looking after the office and acting as communicator and orderly for a detachment of the Brecknock Regiment. Extracts from his diary give some idea of what life was like over the following twelve months:

24 January 1918 – Caught a snake 18 inches long outside guard tent. Natives killed it. Knee still giving trouble –several spells of sick leave.

March 1918 – Scarlet fever among the men.

5 March 1918 – Admitted to hospital, suspected malaria.

7 March 1918 – Cable at noon from Ede with glad news of our baby boy being born, was delighted, not half.

7 April 1918 – Only one letter and paper in the mail, quite disappointed after writing five weeks but later mail arrived noon. Four

letters from Ede, one from mum, two from Fred and one from Annie (sister in law) Quite a treat. Happy as a lark now.

19 April 1918 – In concert at YMCA. I sang 'Anchored' – no one fainted.

14 May 1918 – Recurrence of knee problem after football.

19 May 1918 – Whit Sunday – went to Bible Class and church but my thoughts were more on home than on the sermon.

23 May 1918 – Joined choir at Wesleyans.

9 June 1918 – Letters from Ede, Mother and Fred, all good news except that John has not been heard from for five weeks.

20 June 1918 – Letter from Fred says John officially appointed missing in France, quite likely he is a POW.

5 July 1918 – Had a lively night – got up at 2 am – leg covered in bug bites – had a hunt and finished off one that had taken a fancy to me – gave my charpoy a clean and got rid of a few more travelers [*sic*]

7 October 1918 – Celebration of Bulgaria's exit from the war.

11 October 1918 – L/cpl Hart died in hospital – buried the same evening – used to play tennis with him at the YMCA – all places of amusement and the YMCA etc. put out of bounds owing to flu spreading.

13 October 1918 – Couldn't go out of church owing to being out of bounds.

14 October 1918 – QM in hospital also Bill Atkins both with flu.

16 October 1918 – Feeling a bit seedy. Got feverish so sent to hospital at tea time. My temperature then was 103.6.

17 October 1918 – Had a good sweat in the morning – down to 90 and felt much better – hospital full of flu victims on milk diets.

18 October 1918 – Temperature normal so doc said I could leave the hospital and go to barracks but stay indoors for a while.

The diary stops here.

THE TALE BEHIND THE TALE

Although Charlie's diary is less dramatic than both Fred's and John's, it remains useful to historians studying the war in its entirety. There were perceived threats to British rule in India from inside and outside during both the world wars of the twentieth century and some elements of armed force was needed if only to show a presence. Because the diaries are thorough and detailed, they also allow readers to pick out obvious themes which help us to understand the nature of life for those on what has been described as the 'Forgotten Front'. These themes include danger to health, use of leisure and contact with home.

Danger to Health

It is ironic that those who, in theory, experienced a more comfortable life than their fellows and siblings in the trenches and prison camps 'enjoyed' equally bad health. Many of the great medical developments of the twentieth century came after the First World War and the young Britons, suddenly shipped to a foreign clime, had little in the way of natural bodily defences. Charlie refers to a number of diseases and illnesses including malaria and scarlet fever as well as the dangers presented by various bugs and animals. Above all, there was the infamous influenza outbreak at the end of the war which hit a tired world and took more lives than the war itself. Troops in India were in the front line of this attack. Clearly Charlie had a lucky escape. Many of his fellow soldiers did not.

Research Tip: Accept a Dark Side of War

War is often seen as a case of 'us' and 'them', of 'goodies' and 'baddies'. It is not as simple as that. There are numerous instances of people on the same side falling out, of 'friendly fire' (both intentional and unintentional) and of unrest and even rebellion. Such unrest is worth looking out for when examining an ancestor's experiences. In a number of cases in this book, soldiers are seen to lack respect for officers and feel safer when these officers disappear or are killed. In chapter four, the return to the transport ship after a pleasant stay in Durban led to unease. The ship had been replaced by another one and armed guards with fixed bayonets had to be placed in position to quell any uprising. My father, Rex Gregson, had a similar experience in South Africa in the Second World War. Here, many men were put on a charge for returning late to the vessel and visits to other ports en route to Egypt were cancelled. As in 1917, there was considerable unrest on board. It is only relatively recently that historians have been allowed to be honest about some of the darker sides of war including the large number of casualties caused by friendly fire, accidents and mistakes made in training. In the past, it has also not been 'done' to question morale which, if truth be told, was often low.

A YMCA booklet and a Bilbe from the war, belonging to Charlie.

Use of Leisure

If Charlie's experience of leisure is typical then there seem to be three sub-elements. The first is sport. According to family stories, when his brothers were asked what 'Charles' did in the war, the answer was 'played tennis'. He also played football and cricket and from the diaries it is clear that these two sports, in particular, were both competitive and well organised. In some cases there was even a league system. A second element, linked in some cases to the first, was the Young Man's Christian Association (YMCA), which was a central meeting point for the soldiers where they could play cards and chess and organise their sport. In his diaries, Charlie mentions the boredom which reigned when the local YMCA had to close during the flu outbreak. The YMCA in turn links to the final element, religion. Time allowed for religious practice to be more organised than it was on a more active front. Charlie attended church on a regular basis and was part of a church choir which had time for regular practices. At this point in history, organised religion played a much more central role in British life than it does today. Both Charlie and John, who read the Bible daily in prison camp, were devout Methodists, while Fred, less of a believer, refers to attending the occasional church service on a boat or at the front.

Contact with Home

Charlie wrote letters to all at home. They reached their destination and he in return received letters, cards and even photographs of his newborn son. It would also seem that, on special occasions, he and the family used the telegraph system which he controlled in the office. This contact was something that his brother John in POW camp would have given his eye teeth for, yet it was far from perfect. The mail took weeks to cross and months for a specific question to be answered or request fulfilled. Perhaps the most interesting diary entry here concerns John's fate. Fred was in a position to write and to catch up with his brother in India when on leave at home. Charlie found out in June that John, captured in March, was missing – about the same time that those at home discovered that he was alive and a prisoner of war.

Like a number of the case studies in this book, Charlie's tale is, with minor exceptions, fairly humdrum. This may be true of many who served in the forces during the First World War. Often those behind the more general war effort were also behind the front lines. Ancestors in the navy during the Napoleonic Wars, for example, may have sailed the world for fifteen years or more without seeing action if they were stationed in certain fleets and certain areas. This does not make the study of their experiences less desirable if in some cases they may be less interesting.

5

HAL GREGSON: 'FLYER'S TALE'

My paternal grandfather, Hal Gregson, was a typical product of the Industrial Revolution of the nineteenth century. Born in Barrow-in-Furness in 1894, he was a tinsmith by trade when the war broke out. The Gregsons had worked in the cotton mills of Preston in the early Victorian period before moving to Barrow, a boom town of the late nineteenth century built round steel and shipbuilding. Hal's mother's family, surname Hughes, came from the heart of the Black Country of the Midlands. There they had hewed coal and laboured in the ironworks. According to one of Hal's cousins, their grandfather Hughes had moved to Barrow to 'put the Bessemers in' at the steelworks.

As for many families in the Industrial Revolution, life was hard. By the age of 15, Hal had lost both his parents. They died in their mid-30s. His father had been one of the 'black squad', a boilermaker in the shipyards. Hal was then raised by his mother's sister and at the time of the 1911 census was living with her while serving his apprenticeship.

Hal enlisted in the 4th Battalion of the King's Regiment in November 1915 (No. 3697) and remained in the forces until March 1919 when he was transferred to the reserve. Neither medals nor service overseas are recorded on his discharge certificate. On 29 January 1917, he moved to the Royal Flying Corps and became an airman 2nd class or air mechanic (401423). In March 1918 he was promoted to airman class one and, during the following month, he was 'transferred' into the Royal Air Force at the same rank. In September 1918 he married Annie Selena Greatorex near Oswestry in Shropshire. By the time he was placed on the reserve at RAF Blandford in 1919, he had been promoted to leading airman.

THE TALE BEHIND THE TALE

Although the brevity of this tale may shock some readers, there is a point to it. Researchers into First World War ancestry must be prepared to accept that many wartime careers were fairly uninteresting. The war effort demanded various types of contribution and it was not every man's lot to face death and drama day-in day-out.

I was a teenager at university when my grandfather died. He was an unassuming taciturn man and, to my knowledge, never said much about his war experiences, possibly because they were not particularly interesting and possibly because, with that knowledge in mind, I never quizzed him.

The tale as told is as it stood some thirty years ago when my father and I first researched it. It is based on Hal's demobilisation certificate which we found among his effects plus details gleaned

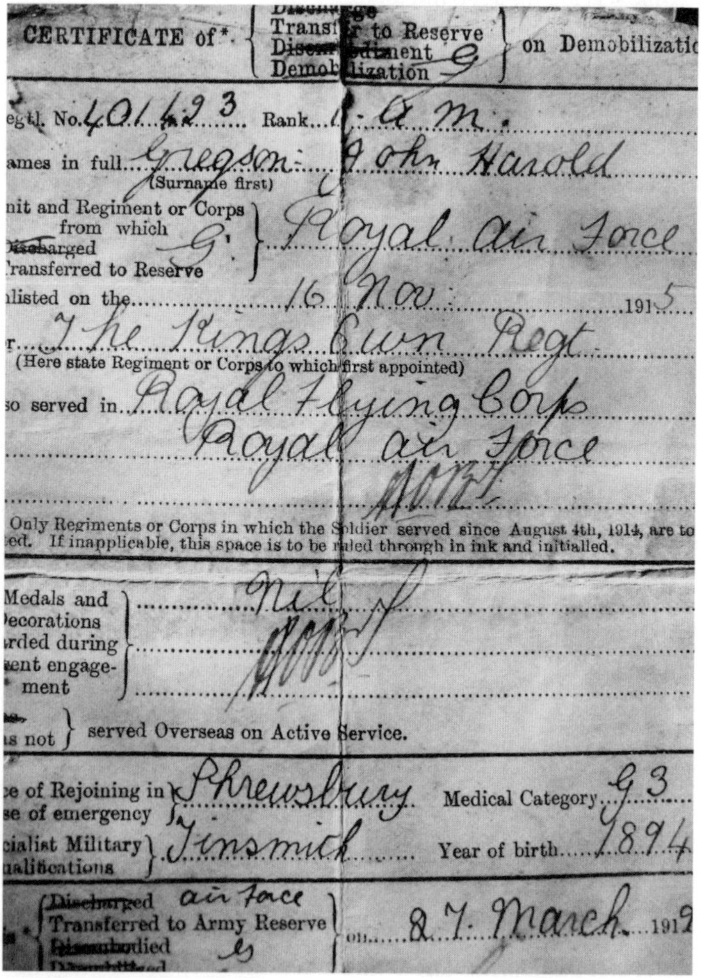

CERTIFICATE of *. Discharge / Transfer to Reserve / Disembodiment / Demobilization G on Demobilizatio[n]

[R]egtl. No. 401123 Rank 1 A. M.

[N]ames in full Gregson: John Harold
(Surname first)

[U]nit and Regiment or Corps from which ~~Discharged~~ G. Transferred to Reserve } Royal air Force

[E]nlisted on the 16 Nov: 1915

[Fo]r The Kings Own Regt
(Here state Regiment or Corps to which first appointed)

[Al]so served in Royal Flying Corps
Royal air Force

Only Regiments or Corps in which the Soldier served since August 4th, 1914, are to [be stat]ed. If inapplicable, this space is to be ruled through in ink and initialled.

Medals and Decorations [awa]rded during [pres]ent engagement } Nil

[Ha]s not } served Overseas on Active Service.

[Plac]e of Rejoining in [ca]se of emergency } Shrewsbury Medical Category G 3

[Spe]cialist Military [Q]ualifications } Tinsmith Year of birth 1894

~~Discharged~~ air force / Transferred to Army Reserve / ~~Disembodied~~ G / ~~Demobilized~~ } on 27 March 1919

Hal's demobilisation certificate.

from the Ministry of Defence after sending them a letter of enquiry. There were also three family photographs. The certificate provided the details outlined in the main tale but also (intriguingly) gave his medical category as G3, a levelling which was not supposed to exist at the time. Whatever the case, it is clear that he was not fit for active service abroad and this tripped a wire in my father's memory that a combination of 'flat feet' and appalling eyesight (Hal wore 'milk-bottle glasses') limited his wartime activities.

The letter from the MOD Departmental Office (archives) was very helpful and polite. It confirmed what was already known and added somewhat to our knowledge of dates. However, as the researching officer pointed out to my father, 'your father's record is over 60 years old and the remaining information is very brief.'

Two of the photographs are of Hal in uniform, one army and one RFC or RAF. The latter photograph was the cause of much amusement in the family. It is of my grandfather and grandmother together before they married. It is signed on the back 'from Flyer'. Apparently his service in the RFC had earned him this nickname and the family joke is that we should have left further detailed research alone and boasted that we had an 'RFC flyer' in the family (even if he would never have been allowed to fly a plane). The other photograph is of the wedding – in fact a double wedding involving my grandmother's younger sister too. A number of the men are in uniform, smiling and smoking large cigars. By September 1918, they were probably aware that the war was nearing an end.

Although my grandfather's war was fairly uneventful, I wondered whether any of the online sites which have grown up over the last thirty years could help me in further fleshing out his wartime career. The three major record groups, service records, pension records and medal rolls, all drew blanks. However, two websites, the Long Trail and the online site of the Kings Own

A soldier's wedding: Hal Gregson (groom) and Billy Gregson.

Royal Regiment Museum, have both proved helpful in providing further details of his army career as well as confirming how his marriage came about.

A detailed examination of his army photograph confirmed that he joined the King's Own Royal Lancaster Regiment. The battalion in which he served was formed at Blackpool in early 1915. Soon after Hal joined, it amalgamated with another battalion and in April 1916 became the 4th Reserve Battalion and moved to Oswestry. There are photographs on the museum site of men and officers at Park Hall Camp, Oswestry in early 1917. Prior to the First World War, my great-grandfather Daniel Greatorex had been head gamekeeper at the hall. During the war, it had been turned over to the military and he had set up a laundry at the camp staffed by his wife and daughters. Clearly Hal had met my grandmother while stationed at the camp and returned later to marry her. By then he had moved out of the army into the air force and his old battalion had been moved out of Park Hall and across to Ireland.

At the time of his marriage, Hal gave his address as 'Yate, Bristol'. There was an RFC/RAF camp there in the First World War and a local history website displays a photograph of a large hangar there filled with camp beds. The airfields of Britain Conservation Trust site reveals that RFC/RAF Yate was formed in March 1917 and remained active in one capacity or another until after the Second World War. The RAF Cricket Association website also has a photograph of an RAF team from Yate in 1918 with one of the players looking remarkably like my grandfather. An online family historian whose ancestor served at Yate also wrote:

> The airfield at Yate, South Gloucestershire, began as No 3 Aircraft Repair Depot originally occupied by the Royal Flying Corps who later became part of the RAF. The repair depot was built by local German POWs and was occupied between 1917 and 1920. The depot had 800 workers, of which 400 were WRAF, working on aircraft maintenance.

All this makes sense. The official forms in our possession mention Hal's trade as 'tinsmith' and, despite my ignorance as to the practice of repairing First World War aircraft, I presume a tinsmith may have been of some use.

We finish with a touching family tale which links Hal with my other grandfather, Fred Stephens (chapter one). Both played for the same football team after the war. Hal was a postman and Fred a counter clerk and they represented Barrow GPO in the Wednesday League. Although Hal had seen no action in the war, he seems to have come out of it the worse of the two physically. He suffered greatly with circulation problems due to the puttees he had to wear as part of the uniform. Prior to each match, Fred used to bandage Hal's legs carefully to protect them.

(Hal did not need shin pads as he was in goal.) What makes this part of the tale the more poignant is that this activity took place at least a dozen years before my mother and father met and started going out with each other.

Research Tip: Work Out Medical Categories

Those who research 'Tommies' in the First World War can be sure of discovering a host of differing wartime experiences. Often this is down to the initial placement of the Tommy himself, which in turn could depend upon health. When the Military Service Act was passed early in 1916, the following categories were set up:

A: General Service.
B1: Garrison Service Abroad.
B2: Labour Service Abroad.
B3: Sedentary Work Abroad.
C1: Garrison Service at Home Camps.
C2: Labour Service at Home Camps.
C3: Sedentary Service at Home Camps.

Those who were below 'A' category were described as 'category men'. In general those in the A category were able to march, had good hearing and were able to stand the conditions of active service. Those in B category had little wrong with them in terms of general health and would be able to work on communications for example. The B subcategories dealt with the ability to walk long distances plus sight and hearing with the poorest in this category assigned desk jobs. The C category covered all those whose health would not allow them to go overseas.

6

BILLY GREGSON: TALES
FROM A RACONTEUR

George William 'Billy' Gregson served in the front line on the Western Front during the First World War. He was my great-uncle and the only sibling of Hal Gregson (chapter five). With Hal, he was raised by a maternal aunt after the death of their parents and Billy served as a telegraph boy in the post office in the years before the war. On one occasion during the conflict, possibly on the Somme, it was his turn to fetch water from the river for use by members of his platoon. He set off on what seemed like a lengthy walk through a wood until he eventually reached the river where he deposited his large canvas water carrier. As he did so 'all hell let loose' from the other side of the river in the shape of an enemy bombardment. Without giving it a second thought, he dived into the river and went under. Each time he ran out of breath, he surfaced only to be met by flying shrapnel. After what seemed an eternity, the bombardment came to an end and he crawled onto the riverbank. The wood had been reduced to a smouldering mass, his uniform and the canvas bag had been ripped to shreds and he was in pain – caused mainly by the desperate dive into the water. Slowly he made his way back to the front line, weakening with every step. By the time he reached his section of the trench, he was on his hands and knees. Eventually, Billy's haggard face appeared over the lip of the trench. Beneath it was the face of one of his pals, who was sitting on the floor of the trench, smoking a woodbine. He smiled at Billy, took the 'tab' out of his mouth and queried, 'Where's the ****ing water then, Bill?'

After one tour in the trenches, Billy was wounded badly enough to earn a 'blighty' or journey home. By now he was a seasoned front-line man and knew that he would be treated, turned around and sent back. He was in the marines and he suspected that his destination would be Haslar Hospital in Portsmouth. On landing in England, he was placed on a stretcher on the dockside where he tried to start a conversation with the man on the neighbouring stretcher. When he got no response, he shook him and immediately realised that the man was dead. Noticing from his neighbour's uniform that he was not a front-line soldier, Billy switched tags with him. As a result, he was sent northwards to the Lake District where he was given plenty of time to recuperate. His lengthy stay in the Lakes made him feel that he had 'got one over' on the establishment.

THE TALE BEHIND THE TALE

Billy's tale is another very short tale with a purpose. For many of my generation, the First World War was about stories told by those who had fought in it. The two stories which make up this tale were recounted to me by Billy himself when I was in my early twenties. Those who have read *A Viking in the Family* will have come across Billy already. He stands as a fine example of the family storyteller or raconteur. The five tales I tell about him came from a single session the day before my grandfather's funeral when my father (Billy's nephew) gave me a ten-shilling note and

Research Tip: Beware the 1911 Census

One of the joys of studying First World War ancestry is in being able to refer to the census of 1911. In theory, the vast majority of those living in England and Wales at this time should be traceable to this census via name, address and age and other details that turn up in wartime records and, by process of elimination, also be traceable to wartime records from the census itself. However, personal experience has taught me to be slightly wary of the twenty-first century's first published census. It was the first census which had to be filled in personally by the head of the household (and one of my family spilled a pot of ink over his census form!) The evidence so far from my family is that some heads of household decided to be lenient with the truth. My hold on this is that between 1901 and 1911, the so-called Liberal Reforms had taken place, which benefited many but also brought the State into the daily lives of more and more families. These reforms also came at a cost which would make some people less than keen for the authorities to know too much about them as such knowledge could, in the future, hit them in the pocket. I have thus found discrepancies in name, age and place of birth of family members when set against evidence given to enumerators at earlier censuses and checked against other official documentation. It is certainly worth double-checking.

Billy Gregson, marine, in training (centre).

told me to take his uncle to the pub. I was studying history at university at the time, so I was keen to collect stories. Although I can recall each story with clarity, I strongly suspect that I am now the family storyteller and it is not beyond the bounds of belief that I have embellished these tales at each telling.

On mature reflection, there are a few questions any right thinking researcher would ask about Billy's stories. Why 'possibly' the Somme in the tale of the missing water? If he swapped identity, did he serve the remainder of the war under another identity or did he blame the muddle-up on someone else? If he had stayed for any length of time as his 'alter ego', surely he would have been punished – possibly, under the circumstances of war, even charged with desertion? The only way to find out whether these tales had weight to them was to carry out further research.

Family memorabilia relating to Billy's experiences is very limited as, unfortunately, my link with Billy's side of the family is not a strong one. All we have as helpmeets are three photographs which belonged to my grandfather. One, autographed on the front, is of Billy on his own and in full uniform. On the back someone has written 'G. William Gregson 1914/18 War'. The photograph was taken in Aldershot and he has the single stripe of a lance corporal on his sleeve topped by crossed flags, the signs of a signaller. The second is a photograph of seven men outside a tent with rifles. Billy is at the front. On the back is written 'Private G.W. Gregson 1489 L? or S? D Company second platoon RMLI 1st Reserved Battalion, Naval Camp Blandford'. The final photograph is of twenty or so men in uniform standing outside a large hut. On the back is written 'William Gregson in camp 1914-18 war'. Both the latter photographs were taken by 'Walshams Ltd 60, Doughty St and Provinces'. (These London photographers appear to have been responsible for many official wartime photographs.) In his brother's wedding photographs, Billy is shown with two stripes on his arm topped by crossed flags: a sign that he had been promoted to full corporal.

The three photographs confirm that Billy served in the marines and his appointment as a signaller fits the bill. Like other members of the family featuring in this book, there were links to the Post Office in civilian life; these were likely to lead to a job in communications in the forces. Also as suspected, 'RMLI', as written on one photograph, stands for Royal Marines Light Infantry and puts Billy firmly on the front line. Moving on from here, online research indicated that the best areas for further detail on RMLI activity involve the National Archives and the Royal Marines Museum. The online 'Jack Clegg Memorial Database of Royal Marine WW medals' includes a listing of all who served in the marines in the First World War. Its search engine led me straight to Billy as Private Ply/1489/S, one of only two 'Georges' there. The database is based on material in the National Archives (ADM159/177) and its contents left me with the option of searching at the National Archives or of paying to find the information on the site. For the sake of speed, I chose the latter course.

Billy enlisted in the marines on 14 March 1916 at Liverpool. He was aged 19½ at the time and his next of kin was given as his brother Hal (see chapter five). He was a private in A Company of the Recruit Division at Deal until August 1916 when he was transferred to the Plymouth Division where he was 'signed in' annually until his demob in February 1919. Throughout he is described as being of very good character and satisfactory ability. In this record he was said to be 5ft 7¼in with grey eyes and brown hair and to have a tattoo on his left forearm 'with a ship, a sun and scroll with a sailor's grave, a crown, a cross and an anchor'. He was also described as a labourer, although in 1911, at 15 years old, he had been a telegraphist messenger boy. The same record noted that he joined the British Expeditionary Force (BEF) in France in November 1916 and returned to the UK in February 1917.

The Royal Marines Museum site came up with more evidence based on a number of helpful online articles. One headed 'Identifying RM Service Numbers' indicates that Ply stands for the Plymouth Division of the marines, a term used since the nineteenth century for one of the three grand marine divisions (the other two were Chatham and Deal). The S stands for short service during the First World War. 'Ranks and Insignia' confirms that the single stripe was for a lance corporal and notes that members of the RMLI were known as privates until 1923, when they became known as individual marines. 'How to Find a Royal Marine's Division in the National Archives' points out that in the First World War there were the RMLI (red marines) and the RMA (blue marines).

So Billy Gregson served as a service soldier in the 1st Reserved Battalion of the Plymouth Division of the Royal Marines

Light Infantry. Would his tales stand up when the activities of this battalion were examined? Further general records suggest that the battalion became part of the 63rd Royal Naval Division which was serving in France in late 1916. Just after Billy landed there, the division was heavily involved in the Battle of Ancre, regarded by historians as the final phase of the Battle of the Somme. The marines, on the left flank of the attack, suffered many losses. The battle was named after a river so it is possible that the Ancre was the river of Billy's 'water carrier incident', not the Somme. The division continued to be involved with the 188th Brigade. This battalion stayed in the Somme region into 1917 and the marines were certainly back in the thick of the action in late February 1917 when they suffered further casualties. This may well explain Billy's return home 'injured' on 26 February.

All in all, there is little in official records so far to prove or disprove the stories Billy told me many years ago. He certainly served in France and is likely to have seen action around the Somme. He also returned to the UK after only a few months of active service and at a time when his battalion was suffering casualties. He never returned to the front, which fits in with his tale, but his record of good conduct tends to suggest that either he behaved himself or was never caught for doing his identity-swapping scam!

What does become abundantly clear when researching 'Tommy' ancestry is that anything was possible during the First World War. 'The fog of war' is a clever term and under its blanket anything could happen; individuals could disappear without trace and the cunning might well have been able to slip away without being caught. As to Billy's tales, we will never know how true they are but I remain certain that they will be passed on down the family for generations to come.

7

JOE BENTLEY: A MYSTERIOUS TALE

Joe Bentley was born at South Lynn, Norfolk in 1896. He was the son of Joseph and Eliza Bentley who had moved to Norfolk from Cambridgeshire not long before his birth. His older brother and sister were born in Cambridgeshire while his two younger brothers and sister were born in King's Lynn. When in Cambridgeshire, father Joseph had been a general labourer at the manure works in Ely but by 1901 had moved to the position of a railway train inspector in King's Lynn. Throughout their time in King's Lynn, the family lived in a house in Saddlebow Road. At the age of 15 in 1911, Joe was working as a printer's apprentice.

In November 1914, by now 18 years old, Joe went eastwards to Dereham to enlist in the Norfolk Regiment. The 1/5 Norfolks had been enlisting here since the outbreak of war. The battalion trained for war at Colchester in Essex and in May 1915 joined with the 1/4 battalion and others to form the 163rd Infantry Brigade. Each battalion was 1,000 strong. The brigade undertook further training at Watford in late May. On 29 July 1915, its members boarded SS *Aquitania* for Gallipoli. (The *Aquitania* was a well-known vessel alongside its sister ships the *Mauretania* and the infamous *Lusitania*.)

After stops at the Greek islands of Mudros and Imbros, the brigade became part of the August landings in Gallipoli and on 10 August found itself on the beach at Suvla Bay. The aim of this landing was to attack the Turks on the plain and in the hills and to come in behind those who were pinning down the Anzac troops at Anzac Cove (see chapter one). The area inland from the beach at Suvla Bay was not suited to fighting battles. There were many small fields and trees. The trees were used by snipers as cover and this had already proved costly in terms of life early in the campaign.

A big attack was planned for 13 August but it was decided to send the 163rd Brigade in a day earlier to clear as much of the area as possible in preparation for the main advance. This manoeuvre took place without specific instructions except that the men should advance as far as they could before digging in with the picks and shovels with which they had been provided. The 1/5 Norfolks were on the right flank of the main advance of 12 August. It was one of three battalions in all, making up a strength since considered too feeble for the task in hand. As the line moved forward, muddled instructions caused a gap to be formed between the right and left flanks. The left flank was also held up by machine-gun fire which meant that the 1/5 Norfolks moved rapidly ahead of the others in the line.

The tale of what was supposed to have happened next was recounted by Sir Ian Hamilton, commander of all the forces in Gallipoli, as follows:

Against the yielding forces of the enemy Colonel Sir H. Beauchamp, a bold, self-confident officer, eagerly pressed forward, followed by the best part of the battalion. The fighting grew hotter, and the ground became more wooded and broken. At this stage many men were wounded, or grew exhausted with thirst. These found their way back to camp during the night. But the Colonel, with sixteen officers and 250 men, still kept pushing on, driving the enemy before them. ... Nothing more was ever seen or heard of any of them. They charged into the forest and were lost to sight or sound. Not one of them ever came back.

Thus was created the myth of the 'Vanished Battalion' which has intrigued historians and enthusiasts of military history ever since. Back in England rumour spread that the battalion had disappeared into a cloud and when that cloud arose soon after, there was no sign of the men. During the war, none of the bodies were recovered and the whole incident continued to make the news, as many of the missing had worked on the Queen's Estate at Sandringham, a fact that had afforded the battalion the nickname 'The Sandringham Pals'. Joe Bentley, the young 19-year-old printer from King's Lynn, was in the 1/5 Norfolk Regiment that disappeared on that day, and his death is recorded as 12 August 1915. His name also appears on the Hellas Memorial in Gallipoli.

THE TALE BEHIND THE TALE

The ability to tell the sad tale of Joe Bentley is an object lesson to all interested in family history research. It is a tale which has emerged from a branch of the Gregson family. Hal Gregson's (chapter five) son Geoff married Anne Gant. Her mother, Gladys, was Joe Bentley's younger sister. When Anne died in Barrow-in-Furness in 2010, among her effects was a large suitcase filled

with photographs. Her friend, Colin Kingston, who was responsible for settling her estate, was loath to 'put them in the bin'
and knowing of my interest in history, suggested that I should
take the suitcase and the pictures. A number of the photographs
related to my side of the family but what really interested me,
as a social historian, were the pictures relating to Anne's side of
the family. These stretched back to Victorian times and to King's
Lynn in Norfolk where Anne's family had lived prior to a move
to Barrow-in-Furness. What really stood out here was a series of
photographs from the First World War, some concerning Anne's
father and others concerning her mother's side of the family and,
in particular, young Uncle Joe. There were pictures of Joe as a
young lad with his sisters, in civvies with a note on the back
saying that he 'went to Dereham in November 1914' and another
with him in uniform and with his friends training at Watford in
June 1915. There were also, I thought, post-war pictures of him
being married and settling down, but I was wrong. (Family like-
nesses can be very confusing.)

At first, the penny did not drop. Among the photographs was
one of a headstone with a bush in front of it. It was dedicated
to Anne's grandparents, the mother and father of Uncle Joe.
There was a second photograph of the same stone but I gave
it scant attention. Later, while double-checking, I noted there
was no bush on this photograph and that the bush had in fact
hidden details of young Joe's death in action on 12 August 1915.
It was at this point that prior knowledge kicked in. I was aware
of the August campaign in Gallipoli through research into my
grandfather's activities. A film for television made a decade or
so ago and entitled *All the King's Men* had also left a mark on
me and I remembered that it involved the Norfolk Regiment
and their mysterious disappearance into the mist. To be honest,
the rest was then plain sailing thanks to the wondrous power
of the search engine and the obvious interest already shown in

the event in question by other researchers. The date of his death, the regiment and company, and even his name swiftly provided me with a wealth of information which convinced me without doubt that he was one of the 250 who had 'disappeared'.

Online research reveals that Joe's name appears on a memorial window in All Saint's Church at King's Lynn. His details are on the relevant website's 'Roll of Honour' alongside all the family details I had already collected through census returns and from family pictures. His regimental number 3411 was also given on the site as well as his company ('B' Company) and the name of the printing firm for which he worked, Messrs Watt and Rowe of King's Lynn. The site also suggested that Joe's death has been recorded in three other places – King's Lynn War Memorial, St Michael's War Memorial South Lynn and on the Helles Memorial in Gallipoli. The same site shows the St Michael's record to be in the form of a recently restored wooden panel currently 'searching for a home' while the King's Lynn War Memorial is the standard 'village green/church square' memorial.

The tale of what was thought to have happened at Suvla Bay on 12 August 1915 and what might really have happened is told on numerous websites. The official history of the regiment written after the war turns to the report of the officer in charge of the Graves Registration Unit in Gallipoli, which was written up nearly four years after the event in September 1919. He states that they discovered 180 bodies of the 5th Norfolks but were only able to identify two of them. They were scattered over an area covering a square mile and this was about half a mile behind the enemy front line. A number of the battalion had apparently made it into a local farm where they had been killed. When the farmer had returned to his house he found the decomposing bodies and disposed of them in a nearby ravine. The received truth is that the battalion became separated from the rest of the rather thin line in the misty conditions and its members were

The Bentley family gravestone (without the bush).

IN LOVING MEMORY OF
ELIZA BENTLEY,
DIED 19TH APRIL 1929,
AGED 63 YEARS.
ALSO OF JOSEPH WILLIAM,
BELOVED HUSBAND OF ABOVE
DIED 22ND MAY 1934,
AGED 74 YEARS.
AND OF JOSEPH WILLIAM,
9TH NORFOLKS, SON OF ABOVE
KILLED IN ACTION
12TH AUGUST 1915.

Joe Bentley and members of the 'lost Norfolks' in training.

picked off one by one in the open. Those that made it into the farm may have been shot by the Turks to spare the problem of keeping them as prisoners.

Whatever the truth behind the tale of the 'Vanished Battalion', it remains one of the great myths of the First World War, now talked of alongside the legendary tale of the 'Angels of Mons' from the early days of the conflict. As noted above, it was further etched into modern memory (and certainly into mine) by the much heralded feature-length BBC film starring David Jason which was first aired on Remembrance Day 1999. *All The King's Men* focussed on the 1/5 Norfolks' links with the Sandringham Estate and on one of the memorials Joe Bentley's name appears alphabetically next to one of the Beck family and the two Batterbee brothers who were featured heavily in the feature film.

Once this book is completed, Joe's wartime memorabilia will be forwarded to his regimental museum. Thanks to Colin Kingston's appreciation of all things historical an interesting and valuable piece of First World War history has been saved.

8

JOE GREATOREX (1891–1980): A CASUALTY'S TALE

When Joe Greatorex enlisted in the King's Shropshire Light Infantry (KSLI) in November 1915 he was 25 years old, a married man and a crack shot. Up until the middle of the nineteenth century, the Greatorex family had worked the land in and around the Derbyshire village of Alvaston for over 400 years. Joe's grandfather, Thomas, had developed wanderlust and eventually became a gamekeeper. He trained Joe's father Daniel in the same occupation. Joe was born near Lingfield Racecourse in Surrey but spent his youth on various estates scattered around Britain. When he was 12, his father was head gamekeeper at Stoke Edith in Herefordshire, in charge of ten men. Family photographs from this period show young Joe carrying a gun even at this tender age. Joe also trained as a gamekeeper and after his marriage in 1912 (see chapter nine) took up a gamekeeper's post at Winchcombe in Gloucestershire. He was here at the time of his enlistment.

Joe served in the 7th Battalion of the KSLI which was formed soon after the outbreak of war, with headquarters at Shrewsbury. A couple of months before he enlisted, the battalion arrived in France and stayed there 'serving entirely on the Western Front' and often in the thick of the action. Over the winter of 1915–16, it was involved in activities around the Ypres Salient before moving on to the Somme for the big offensive of 1916. The battalion arrived in the area on the fated 1 July but did not become involved in front-line activity for a couple of weeks. The Battle of Bazentine Ridge began on 14 July and the 7th KSLI was involved in heavy fighting here and in late July and August, taking heavy casualties. The attack on the village of Serre on 13 and 14 November was particularly memorable. Overall 'The 7th' suffered more casualties than any other KSLI battalion during the war, with 1,048 killed in action or dying as a result of injury. It also earned more battle honours than any other KSLI battalion.

By March 1917, Joe had been promoted to corporal and since he was allowed to wear a blue chevron on his uniform, must have seen action for the best part of a year. In March, he was placed in a field hospital suffering from a urine and kidney complaint described as albuminuria (and in Joe's case it was first noted as 'mild'). The disease is also known as 'trench nephritis', one of a number of recognised trench diseases caused by the insanitary conditions in the trenches (rats, decomposing bodies and overflowing latrines). Trench nephritis could be fatal if not dealt with fairly promptly.

As a result of his illness, Joe was placed in No. 6 Stationary Field Hospital at Frevent. This was inland between Dieppe and Beauvais and close to the battlefront. From here, he was moved to the 16th Field Hospital at Le Treport on the coast between Dieppe and Abbeville. This was used by British and Commonwealth forces from January 1915 to June 1917 when it was taken over by US forces. Le Treport was a staging post for those who were on their way back to Britain for treatment. On 17 March 1917, Joe landed in Portsmouth en route for hospital treatment at Duston, Northampton, where he arrived on the following day.

After recovering from his illness, Joe was transferred to the 3rd (special reserve) Battalion KSLI which had started life as the county militia. It was purely a training battalion and saw no overseas war service. The 3rd KSLI served in Scotland and Wales and moved to Cork in Southern Ireland in December 1917, ending its role in the war at Fermoy. During this period, Joe served in Ireland as a Lewis Gun Instructor First Class and received promotion to sergeant. He returned to Winchcombe and his role as a gamekeeper in 1919.

THE TALE BEHIND THE TALE

Joe Greatorex was my great-uncle, the younger brother of Annie Selena and thus brother-in-law to Hal Gregson (chapter five). Unfortunately I only met him on a couple of occasions and did not discuss his wartime activities with him during his lifetime. He did, however, correspond on family history matters in general and, when he died, I was passed his collection of war memorabilia. After the war, Joe became something of a national celebrity in the field of gun-dog breeding and field trials. During the Second World War, he served as a colour sergeant in the Royal Welsh Fusiliers and used his expertise as a marksman to train the Home Guard. (There are documents relating to this experience too.)

As a result of Joe's 'fame', the local and specialist press covered his retirement and eventual death. Of his war record, the *Shropshire Journal* noted on his retirement in 1964:

Research Tip: Watch out for a Confusion of Names

There is a trick quiz question that asks 'What is Paul McCartney's first name?' As is fairly common knowledge, the former Beatle was christened James Paul McCartney but opted to use his 'middle' name as his preferred Christian name. This is not in the least uncommon and it can cause problems for the family history researcher, especially when they wish to consult extensive indexes. Take the two Gregson brothers who form the subject matter of chapters five and six. They were known in the family as Hal and Willie. Hal was christened John Harold Hughes Gregson; John after his paternal grandfather and Hughes after his mother's maiden surname. In records he appears as John while the 'Hughes' part of his name does not appear on any of his war records. Willie was christened George William – George after both his father and great-grandfather. He appears under George in most records. Joe Greatorex, subject of this chapter, was christened Thomas Joseph Greatorex, after his grandfather and great-grandfather, and appears in the medal card records as Thomas J. Greatorex. Thomas Arthur Watterson (chapter nineteen) was known as 'Artie'. My mother was christened Betty. This is not a shortening for Elizabeth as is normal practice, but she can be found under E. Gregson in some official records. My mother's cousin Joan was Joan all her life, though christened Hilda Joan and annoyingly called Hilda by those treating her in old age. My father was christened John Daniel Rex Gregson; John after his father's (rarely used) first surname, Daniel after his maternal grandfather and Rex after the last three letters of his mother's surname (Greatorex).

> He was known as Rex all his life. Thus it can be amusing when genealogy 'pay sites' try to inveigle me into their system by asking if either of my 'John Gregsons' were war heroes! In researching ancestry it pays to be dogged in looking at different ways officialdom may have noted down 'real' names.

When the 1914–18 War intervened, Mr Greatorex served with the 7th Battalion K.S.L.I. and, being a keen shot was soon a small arms instructor. He was promoted to sergeant and served in France.

On Joe's death in 1980, gun-dog expert Peter Moxon wrote:

> In 1915 he joined up in the Shropshire Light Infantry and served until 1917 when he was invalided home with nephritis from which he nearly died. Subsequently he served in Southern Ireland as a sergeant, returning to his keepering job at the cessation of hostilities.

Such obituaries are worth looking out for if an ancestor had something of a local reputation. Around the time of his death, a letter written to me by his niece confirmed his service in Ireland towards the end of the war.

Joe's wartime material embraces a number of valuable and informative documents including a large number relating to his illness (see chapter nine). One of the most interesting is a pocket-sized booklet running to seventeen pages issued to members of the 7th Battalion KSLI exclusively in January 1917 and bearing the title 'Trench Standing Orders'. It is packed with information about expected behaviour in the trenches and gives us some idea of 'good habits' picked up over more than two years of attritional warfare. The index covers fifteen subheadings such as sanitation, wiring parties, gas and discipline. Perhaps one of the most poignant, not to say slightly amusing, sections is entitled 'Care of Feet' and runs as follows:

> The following precautions against Trench Feet will be taken in the winter months:-
>
> On the day the battalion proceeds to the Trenches, Companies will hand in to their Quartermasters one dirty pair of socks per man, receiving in exchange one clean pair per man. Thus each man will go up to the Trenches with one clean pair of socks on, and one in the haversack. During the first night, each man will again change his socks, and one pair of socks per man will be sent to the Quartermaster under arrangements to be made with Battalion Headquarters. Clean socks will be brought up in exchange the following night. The same process will be continued during the tour. When returning dirty socks, Company Commanders will render a certificate as to a) No. of socks drawn the previous night. B) No. of socks returned.
>
> Each man will have his feet well rubbed with whale oil before proceeding to the Trenches.
>
> Boots will be taken off once daily, during which time whale oil will be rubbed into the feet.

In fact, feet care was no laughing matter as Trench Foot (an advanced and nasty form of athlete's foot) could turn a soldier into a casualty. The threat of Trench Foot was even regarded as a genuine problem in the Falkland's War of the late twentieth century.

A thin handwritten sheet of paper also contains details of Joe's 'wages' when in the forces. Between November 1915 and September 1916, he received 17s 6d per week. From then until January 1917 this went up to a straight £1 (a rise of just over

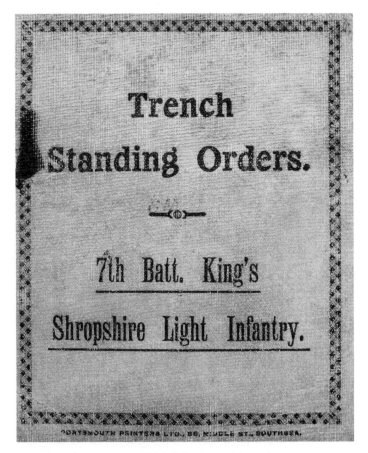

Trench Standing Orders for KSLI belonging to Joe Greatorex.

15 per cent) and in the middle of February he was given a postal order for 8s to cover a further increase.

Army Form Z18 given out at the time of demobilisation and entitled 'Certificate of Employment during the War' is fairly detailed on his wartime career. 'The object of this certificate,' its author noted, 'is to assist the soldier in obtaining employment on

Private Broughton's letter to Joe Greatorex.

his return to civil life.' The document gives regimental number, name and rank, regiment and unit as well as regimental employment, trade or calling before enlistment, courses of instruction and certificates, military qualifications and special remarks. It was signed by the commanding officer of the 'unit'. Joe's certificate is not as detailed as it might be as it has a line drawn through regimental employment and special remarks. The commanding officer would have many of these to complete and may have been inclined to 'reel them off' as swiftly as possible. Joe's form is useful in informing us of his Lewis gun expertise (courses, certificates and military qualifications) and in providing the information that he ended the war in the 3rd KSLI after initially serving in the 7th Battalion.

Perhaps the most interesting document in Joe's wartime memorabilia is a letter written on YMCA headed notepaper. It tells an intriguing tale and also presents the researcher with a mystery that may never be solved. The letter is from a Private W. Broughton 3955 of A Company 315 Cheshire Regiment stationed at Whittington Camp, Shropshire. It reads:

> Dear Mr Greatorex just a few lines to let you know how I went on after falling out of the train on Saturday Well will you kindly drop me a few lines and make it out as a witness for me they asked me if I was drunk and I told them not but thay cud not believe me so I told them that I ad you for a witness so try and do your best for me I avent dun mutch as myself I of only cut my head and back I think I must have been asleep and walked out in my sleep so if you tell them that I walked out in my sleep I think I shall get of but send me a line as soon as you can

On the other side of the letter is what appears to be a reply in Joe's handwriting. It reads:

> I was travelling on the same train and in the same compartment as Private W Broughton when he stepped out of the train. He was perfectly sober and opened the door thinking no doubt we were in Shrewsbury Station and before he could recover from his mistake, the speed of the train threw him between the next pair of metal ?? (Unclear) … It was a pure accident. The man did this quite innocently and if he is punished it will be an injustice to him. I know nothing of this man but hope that this will clear him as I said he was perfectly sober and did it quite accidentally.

Unfortunately there is no date on the letter and even if there were, the incident appears to have been too minor to have appeared in a local newspaper anyway. Perhaps the addressing of Joe as Mr Greatorex indicates that this took place prior to his enlistment (but then again he may have been in 'civvies' as he was close to his parental home; Whittington Camp was Park Hall Camp, where his mother and sisters ran the laundry).

Research Tip: Be Aware of Censorship

A number of the primary sources used in this book were censored at the time or refer to censorship in passing. The most interesting perhaps is the letter sent from Fred Stephens (chapter one) to his mother in 1915 when he was en route for Gallipoli. In this letter both the destination of the vessel and the number of soldiers on board has been cut out and the term 'incision by censor' applied. In letters and cards sent home by those in hospital and those who were prisoners of war, the writers were often limited to crossing out sentences which did not apply to their circumstances. Any signs of extra additions would have led to the missive home being destroyed. Official stamps on letters from prisoners of war indicate that what they wrote was read by both the Germans and the British. This is another reason why such letters and cards took a long time to reach their destinations. The censors looked to eliminate anything which gave factual information on the movement of forces or provided evidence of low morale. When intelligence was being collected from the enemy in the trenches, the collectors were seeking out evidence of areas which were weak and good to attack due to the inexperience and low morale of the troops occupying them.

There are a couple of William Broughtons in the records who served with the Cheshire Regiment but neither bears his regimental number, 3955. One of them was killed in action near Ypres in October 1917 and has had his career researched and placed online by students at Whitby High School, Ellesmere Port.

At least two of Joe's brothers served in the forces. Harry was a sergeant in the Warwickshire Regiment from the onset of war and was wounded. Charlie served as a sergeant with the KSLI on the front from 1915 and was also wounded by a German bayonet. According to one family story, Joe was on sentry duty in Ireland when it happened and felt the stab. When the brothers met after the war, they confirmed that the timing of this happening was correct.

By the end of the war, Joe had been made a sergeant too and one suspects that all these promotions may have been linked to their experiences with guns as young men with a gamekeeper father. Events surrounding Joe's illness on the front and consequent activity are dealt with separately in the next chapter.

9

GERT GREATOREX: THE TALE
OF A CASUALTY'S WIFE

Gert Greatorex (*née* Evans) was the daughter of a game-keeper, brought up beside the canal at Llangollen within sight of the famous canal viaduct across the River Dee. In 1912, she married Joe Greatorex (chapter eight) who was a gamekeeper himself at nearby Ruabon. Soon after their marriage, they moved to Winchcombe in Gloucestershire where Joe took up a post as gamekeeper. They had a daughter in 1915, the same year as Joe enlisted in the King's Shropshire Light Infantry. While he was on the front line, Joe was able to write to and receive letters from his wife. When he was struck down by kidney disease in late February or early March 1917 he kept Gert informed of both his condition and movements, with occasional help from officialdom.

Gert knew that Joe was in reasonable health on 11 February 1917, as he sent her a standard form postcard noting that he was 'quite well' and that he had recently received a letter from her to which he hoped to reply in the near future. The first news of his illness came from the regimental barracks at Shrewsbury. This was sent on 8 March 1917, and was received by Gert a few days later. It told her that Joe had been placed in the field hospital near to the front and described the nature of his illness. It also promised to keep her updated on his progress. The next communication to arrive was an undated official postcard with details of his move to a coastal hospital and slightly more information on the nature of his illness. Around the same time Gert also received a letter apparently from Joe himself and written on 7 March from the coastal hospital:

Dearest Gert, a thought you was wondering and getting anxious as towards become of me you have no cause to worry at tall soon may matter a week or a fortnight till I land in England no dought you will wonder of this writing for me that a must be very bad not to be able to write a few lines myself it is only on account of the strength of my eyes that sister will not let me write myself whatever you do do not start to write yourself as it is only a couple of weeks till I land in England trusting you are all in the best of health looking forward to seeing you all in nearest future [indecipherable sentence]

With fondest love and kisses from your loving Joe

And four days later, she received this from the same hospital:

My dear Gert,

Just a line or two more trusting they will find yourself and Babs are all quite [well?] am pleased to say I am fine … Felt better today and yesterday than I have done since first it started And the swelling is … down fine and I could write quite normal only it is awkward job writing ones clinical charts in this ? Keep on like this and I should be over in a very few days. About twice a week they send men across. It takes a couple of days – but the trains etc are fine with this. Failing? Still in food been for a feed when the time comes Diet at present – 4.30 a.m. hot milk 7.30 milk hot 10.30 hot milk 12.30 Milk hot 1.30 Bar of Chocolate 4.30 Hot Milk .30 Hot Milk 8.30 Lemonade

12-3-17 May birthday today – no letter from me for her … Rained most of the night here

Fondest love from your loving husband, Joe.

This letter was passed by the censor on 14 March.

On 17 March 1917, Joe wrote a card and posted it in Portsmouth:

Landed this side all right and are now on our way to some hospital in Northampton. Will write to you as soon as possible on arrival there. Having a fine journey. Lovely day. Pleased to be in dear old blighty again. Hope all is well. Fondest love, Joe

On the following day, a card was posted to Gert from Northampton War Hospital at Duston with Joe's personal army details in his own handwriting on one side and details of the support available to visitors for travel on the other.

Around the same time, Gert received notice that she was to receive more money in her separation allowance 'on account of the new scale for children under fourteen years of age'. This was to be cashed through a separate postal draft until April 1917 when the new scale would be incorporated in the general separation allowance. Towards the end of the war there is also evidence of her using rationing cards for herself and her daughter.

THE TALE BEHIND THE TALE

As in the case with 'Lil' Stephens (chapter three), material left by
a soldier allows us to get an overview of life for the wife at home.
In this case, it also enables us to compare the experiences of a
woman with a hospitalised husband to that of one whose partner
was a prisoner of war. The person concerned was my great-aunt
through marriage.

Among Joe's memorabilia is Army Form w183, the so-called
'next of kin card', addressed to Gert at their Winchcombe home
and sent in November 1915 when he enlisted. It names her as
next of kin to be informed if anything happened to her husband and lists the KSLI headquarters at Shrewsbury as her point
of contact.

It is also worth looking at the written material relating to
Joe's illness which gives some idea as to how the next of kin
were kept informed. Joe's last correspondence before the illness
was on a standard Field Service postcard (A.F.A. 2042 114/Gen
no/5249). Most of the information on this card was typed and
information passed on to the recipient only by the crossing out
of printed text where not applicable. It was noted in print that
the card would be destroyed if the writer wrote more than the
recipient's address on one side and his signature and date on the
other. On the envelope of a later letter Joe has to affirm by his
signature that 'on his honour … the contents of this envelope
refer to nothing but private and family matters'.

Official notification of Joe's illness came from Shrewsbury on
Army Form B 104-80A. It was signed by a second lieutenant on
behalf of the colonel in charge of records based at the barracks.
There were three rubber stamps on it: 'Casualty Branch',
'Infantry Record Office, Shrewsbury' (and date) and 'King's
Shropshire Light Infantry'. The form provided details of the
first field hospital he was in. An undated 'Hospital Redirection

Card' (Army Form A.2042) followed and was one which had to be filled in and forwarded to the next of kin upon the casualty's admission. It had stamps on the front marked '16 General Hospital' and 'Army Post Office S13'. It also has the number 35 handwritten in the top left corner, which later proved to be the ward Joe was in. In both of the latter cases, the hospitals were easy to trace on online sites dedicated to the history of the war.

The two letters which arrived from Joe while in the coastal field hospital were written on plain paper. The first one was clearly dictated as it states thus and is not in Joe's handwriting. The poverty of the English also suggests that it was written down by somebody else, a nurse, a volunteer or perhaps another patient. The second letter is in Joe's hand. It was on a folded piece of paper with the address on one side and two stamps marked 'Passed Field Censor 2099' and 'Army Post Office 14 March 1917'. The postcard sent upon landing in England was a standard civilian one but had 'Sick Soldier Postcard' on the front to avoid

Joe Greatorex's 'next of kin' card.

the payment of postage. He wrote it at 1 p.m. and it was stamped 5.45 p.m. on the same day. On this card he refers to 'Babs' (his baby daughter) and to his younger sister May.

The card sent on his arrival at the war hospital at Duston is an interesting one. Headed 'official army form W3229', it was to 'serve as the official notification' to the 'next of kin'. It had the address of the recipient on the front as well as the name,

Research Tip: Look out for Non-Combat Casualties

One of the surprises when studying the First World War comes when calculating the number of casualties that are not as a direct result of combat. Joe Greatorex (chapters eight and nine) was lucky to survive trench nephritis, a potentially fatal disease that attacked the kidneys. Other trench diseases to look out for include trench foot and trench fever. Fred Stephens (chapter one) and a number of his friends suffered from the heat in Gallipoli and had to be removed from the combat zone. Fred also lost his teeth and his appendix. Charlie Stephens (chapter four) survived the great influenza epidemic at the end of the war. Many of his friends did not. Charlie was in India and also had a slight touch of malaria. Young (and not so young) Britons who served in foreign climes often did not have the natural defences to fight disease and preventative medicine still had a long way to go. Fred Stephens again (chapter one) lost his dear friend Sandy Bayne to disease contracted in Mesopotamia. As a history teacher in the 1980s, I noted with fascination that the end of the Falklands' conflict came just in time as many of the soldiers on land were beginning to suffer from trench foot.

Dictated letter from Joe Greatorex in a French hospital.

rank, number and regiment of the patient. On the other side was printed the heading 'Railway Facilities for visiting Soldiers in Hospital in the United Kingdom' and the details here are extremely informative. It notes that one relative, and one only, could get a travel voucher if the patient was in a grave condition and the relative was unable to afford the fare. If the visit was urgent, a telegram from the MO would allow for a later refund of travel costs. Vouchers were also available for return fares for the cost of a single fare as long as the journey took place within 30 miles of the hospital. These vouchers could be applied to two adults or one adult and two children under the age of 12. Only one visit was allowed under this scheme although medical officers did have discretion and relatives were asked to deal through these officers alone in all matters relating to their transport to and from hospital.

Even more valuable perhaps both in tracing activities on the Home Front and in progressing family history in general was the information given on the front of the envelopes and on the address sides of the postcards. The initial next-of-kin card written in 1915 gave the family address as Woodbine Cottage, Corndean, Winchcombe, Gloucestershire. Joe's 'quite well' postcard was sent here. So too, initially, was the official notification from Shrewsbury that he had been taken ill. However, there are three postage stamps on the address side of this folded letter – Shrewsbury 9 March, Winchcombe 10 March and Oswestry 11 March. The Winchcombe address has also been crossed out and replaced by 'Park Hall Laundry, Oswestry, Salop', indicating perhaps that Gert and her daughter were paying a visit to her in-laws at the time Joe fell ill (see chapter five).

From this time onwards, correspondence from Joe and relating to his illness was addressed to 'No 2, Canal Terrace, Vronneysyllte, Llangollen' with Vronneysyllte (modern spelling Froncysyllte) shortened to Vron on a couple of occasions. This, at first, seemed rather confusing but internet research soon sorted out the problem. This was effectively Gert's family home. Using the *Genealogist* search engine for addresses, I discovered Gert here in 1911 with her widowed mother. This was just before her marriage to Joe. Looking back to the 1901 census, I discovered a younger Gert with her mother and gamekeeper father. This possibly explains how she had first come across her gamekeeper future husband. As with Lil Stephens (chapter three), the married Gert had returned to the bosom of the family in time of crisis, only in her case it was to be with a blood relative rather than an in-law.

Hidden among the written material were also two little rationing tickets (for sugar). One was in Gert's name and one in the name of her daughter Margaret Elizabeth. Both were dated

June 1918 and had been cancelled and signed off at Winchcombe, an indication that they had returned home and were able to celebrate with something sweet.

I met Great-Aunt Gert on a couple of occasions. Like her husband, she was well known and apparently much loved in the world of gun-dog shows and field trials. Her lengthy obituary in *Shooting Times* indicates that she was known to all in the gundog world simply as 'Mother'.

10

JANET DAWSON: THE TALE
OF AN ARMY NURSE

Janet Dawson was born in the coastal village of Haverigg in Cumberland in 1892. She was the daughter of the village joiner and undertaker. At the age of 18, she went to work as a nurse in a hospital at Ilkeston in Derbyshire and received training in the areas of accident and surgery. Three years later, she moved near home to the Cumberland Infirmary in Carlisle. Here she worked as a probationary nurse for three years and a staff nurse for one.

During her probationary period at the Cumberland Infirmary, Janet was involved in caring for those who were injured as a result of the Quintinshill or Gretna Green Rail Disaster which took place on 2 May 1915. It is still described as 'Britain's worst rail disaster' with over 200 killed, many of them soldiers on the way to active service. Over 200 more were injured as three trains were involved in this single incident. Janet was rushed to the scene in a horse-driven cart and her full story relating to the event is told in *A Viking in the Family*. Such was the effect of the disaster that gas lighting was banned from carriages and carriages themselves had to be constructed from metal. Many of the victims had burned to death.

By May 1917, Janet was working as a nurse in a Voluntary Aid Detachment Hospital in Carlisle, caring for the wounded brought back from the front. She was keen to make her service more useful and permanent and thus applied by letter to join the Queen Alexandra's Imperial Military Nursing Service Reserve – the QAIMNS(R). She filled in a detailed application form and added the names of three referees. Early in the following month, she had her application accepted but wrote to say that her contract with the Carlisle hospital was for four years and did not run out until September 1917, when she would be able to 'join up'. The hospital was prepared to let her go in July but by September she was home in Haverigg and writing letters in frustration to the Chief Matron of the uniformed service complaining that she was now at home kicking her heels. The reply from the matron's office suggested that she found some 'temporary work'. Janet responded saying that temporary work was difficult to find, and within two weeks she was told that her place in the QAIMNS(R) was ready for her.

On 19 October 1917 Janet was told to report to the Military Hospital at Woking. The letter of instruction included a rail warrant and a guarantee that she would receive £8 on arrival 'for uniform'. She arrived at Woking on 24 October 1917, two days after writing to the Chief Matron once more to confirm that she was coming. Her father had already acted as witness on a form where she had agreed to serve 'so long as required'. The same form included all the arrangements for pay, work and travel. Janet worked at the Woking hospital until the end of March 1919 under the command of the military regime at Aldershot.

During this period she met and nursed her future husband, South African army officer William Thomas (see chapter eleven), and was described as a staff nurse (2 Res D/279). She was demobbed as a result of an urgent request from the Hythe nursing home in Kent that she be released. This request was met with immediately. She was paid up to the end of the month, had her NH Insurance arrears updated (75 weeks at 3*d* a week) and was sent off with a gratuity. Her demobilisation report was signed by her matron who noted that she served for one year and five months and that her work had been 'satisfactory' and her conduct 'good'.

After the war she moved to South Africa and married William Thomas but his early death brought her back to England. After the death of her husband (see chapter eleven), she wore her nursing badge alongside his two service medals on Armistice Day. All three medals are now in my possession.

THE TALE BEHIND THE TALE

Janet Dawson (later Thomas and ultimately Stephens) was my step-grandmother and a lady I knew well, our relationship continuing into my own married lifetime. She married twice, first to South African William Thomas (chapter eleven) who died in the 1920s, then to my grandfather Fred 'Pop' Stephens (chapter one). 'Pop' and Janet had been childhood friends in Millom, Cumberland. By the early 1930s, both were widowed and raising daughters. What seemed a marriage of convenience in fact worked very successfully. My mother, still alive today and in her nineties, lived with her from the age of 13 until her marriage.

Janet did not talk much about her experiences in the war years. The story of her Gretna Green Tragedy, told in *A Viking in the Family*, was pieced together mainly from family memory.

My mother recalled that her stepmother went out to the scene of the accident on a cart while I remember her saying that she had nothing to hand to work with apart from neat Jeyes' Fluid. While the current book was being prepared, my mother told me that a young doctor had asked Janet to give him a hand with an injured victim. As she tried to lift the patient, one of his legs came off in her hand. I suspect that my mother had kept that story back, reluctant to tell her son a tale so macabre until he was in his sixties. (A lesson to us all to keep on probing aged relatives even when we think we've got all the information there is.)

The family was obviously aware that Janet had nursed in Carlisle in 1915 but had little idea of what happened thereafter. My mother seemed to think that her stepmother had met her first husband while nursing him somewhere in the south, possibly at Aldershot, and that she may have been 'an army nurse'. This is backed up by a tale Janet once told me when we were watching a cricket match between England and Australia on the television. She suddenly observed that she had nursed Australians during the First World War and that they had been 'real terrors', always misbehaving and refusing to stay in their beds. I mentioned this to my mother recently and she remembered being told that a group of Australians once picked up a nurse and dumped her unceremoniously in an empty bath. Yet another new tale!

The possibility of an army nursing career for Janet needed to be explored if she was to feature in this book and an entry into a search engine led directly to the National Archives and 'Looking for the records of a British Army Nurse – What do I need to know before I start?' The recommendations were: a name, the name of the service and a geographical location and date range 'to help focus' the search. I chose Janet Dawson and entered this name into the search engine for series WO 399, that is for those who served in the Queen Alexandra's Imperial Military Nursing

Service, the Queen Alexandra's Imperial Military Nursing Service (Reserve) and the Territorial Force Nursing Service during the First World War. If successful I would discover:

Where she trained (especially before the war).

References relating to her suitability as a military nurse.

Hospitals, field ambulances, casualty clearing stations or other medical units she served in.

What her superiors thought of her (confidential reports).

When she left the services.

The National Archives guide also noted that the majority of these records were written out on pre-printed army forms, which were then completed in ink or pencil. The only items not on army forms were the references and any personal letters from the specific individual to the War Office or to the army nursing authorities. There was only one Janet Dawson on the index (reference: WO 399/2124), so I duly paid a small fee online and within a few minutes had thirty-plus pages of digitised primary source material in front of me. Even the briefest scanning of this material told me I had the right person and would thus be able to tell the tale of her wartime activities. Using the headings above I was able to complete Janet's case study as follows.

Where She Trained

Looking in particular at where she trained before the war. This was on a Queen Alexandra's Imperial Military Nursing Service Reserve form of application which she signed on 18 May 1917. This referred to her education at Millom High School and details of her pre-war training at Ilkeston and both her training and employment at the Cumberland Infirmary before and during the war. Her presence at Ilkeston in 1911 was backed up by a look at the relevant census entry for the hospital.

References
These were those relating to her suitability as a military nurse. The names of referees were on the same form but none of the references were attached.

Establishments She Served With
Including hospitals, field ambulances, casualty clearing stations or other medical units she served in. Her wartime service at Woking Military Hospital was covered by an official form dated 22 May 1917. It had her official registration number at the top and was initialled by various people without comment up until 4 June 1919, when it was stamped 'closed'.

Confidential Reports
In other words, what her superiors thought of her. This consisted of her final character reference alone.

When She Left the Services
There was detailed information on length of time served and date of termination, of pay, of the gratuity awarded, and National Health Insurance payments made. Much of the information was under the heading 'Nurses temporarily employed by the Q.A.I.M.N.S' and referring to her personal reference number, 2 Res D/279, and position as staff nurse.

Other Information
As the National Archives index suggested, much of this information was on official army forms yet, in Janet's case, by far the biggest and most interesting and informative pieces of evidence came in the section of the guide entitled 'personal letters'. Reading these online was quite moving, as the material included a number of letters from Janet herself and I immediately recognised her handwriting from the front of a variety of books she

had given to me with personal dedications. The bulk of these letters (and replies received) covered the period from May to October 1917 when she was having difficulties 'joining up'. Others were formal letters saying that she had 'the honour' of arriving at Woking in 1917 and of leaving in 1919. Other letters were from the office of the Matron-in-Chief on the Thames Embankment, the headquarters in Aldershot, allowing her to demobilise and the nursing home in Hythe requesting that she be demobilised swiftly. She also forwarded Army Form 3537 from home before leaving. This was signed by herself and her father and dealt with a number of matters relating to her wartime employment.

All in all, this was a most satisfactory case to research. I was able to move from mere suspicion that she had been an army nurse to a position where I could piece together a more than useful outline of her service in the forces. This case stands as proof that the evidence can be out there and, thanks to online digitisation, readily available and easy to access and use at home.

11

WILLIAM THOMAS: TALE OF A TRENCH RAID

When W.F.G. Thomas died in Pretoria, South Africa in 1925 at the age of 32, the writer of his obituary in the local newspaper noted that he 'served with honour throughout the war'. William Thomas was South African, born of Cornish stock, and courage seems to have been in his blood. One of his direct ancestors had been awarded a medal for his efforts to save the life of a drowning lighthouse keeper off the Cornish coast and his father, Captain W. J. Thomas, had gained the Distinguished Conduct Medal during the Boer War.

In the early days of the war, William saw action with the Rand Light Infantry in German South West Africa. By the end of 1916, he was a second lieutenant with the 3rd Regiment South African Infantry stationed in the trenches to the north of Arras. In December he was chosen with another officer of the same rank to carry out a trench raid on the German lines. A party of just over fifty men targeted a section of the German trenches 100yd long. The initial aim of this raid was to 'obtain identity prisoners, kill enemy, bomb dugouts if any', but this was later modified slightly to 'capturing prisoners, obtaining identifications, and doing as much harm to the enemy as possible'.

The raid took place in the darkness of a winter's evening so a rope was provided 'for men to hold and keep in touch while going over'. Their faces were smeared with mud and chalk and each man had a luminous patch on his back. This was so their colleagues could recognise them instantly in the dark and not fire on them by mistake. The men were instructed to carry 'no badge of rank, badge, correspondence or name' and to give only rank and name if captured. The party was divided into two groups with Lieutenant Thomas in charge of the left flank. Among the equipment carried were ten duckboards with slats 3in apart. These were to be put across the barbed-wire entanglements in no-man's-land so the men could cross quickly. The officers had a large map and an aerial photograph 'of rather poor quality' to work from while those monitoring the raid from the home trenches were provided with five phones and two runners so the powers-that-be could be kept informed.

Before the raid took place, the enemy trench was put under a barrage of fire from the artillery. Three minutes after the attack started, this barrage stopped and the artillery bombed the German support trenches behind so that reinforcements could not be sent forward to the very front line. At each end of the area attacked, those in the Allied front line gave firing support with machine guns and trench mortars.

The distance between the two sets of trenches was only 120yd at the point of the raid. Those in the party had three minutes to cross, seven minutes to 'fight, bomb and block' and three minutes to retire. After ten minutes exactly, a Morse message on a French horn blasted out from the home trench – a message repeated by the two officers in charge on the French horns with which they had been provided. A signal rocket was sent off at the same time.

The raid was regarded as a success: 'only one prisoner was brought in but a number of dug-outs and concrete machine-gun emplacements were destroyed and the enemy suffered many casualties.' This single prisoner was sent to 'Candle Factory' for examination and William and his fellow officer were both awarded the Military Cross. Months later, William was severely wounded during the first few minutes of the advance that took place early on the first morning of the Battle of Arras. By the time he left France for hospital in England, he had already been mentioned twice in Haig's own dispatches.

So severely wounded was William Thomas that he did not return to the front. In March 1918, he was moved from second lieutenant to temporary first lieutenant. This position was made permanent in January 1919 although he was to relinquish his commission and return to civilian life in August of the same year.

After the war William Thomas worked in the mining and railway industries but remained interested in military affairs. In 1921, he was officer in charge of an escort for the colours at the time of a royal visit to Pretoria. Days before his sudden death, he was a guest at the funeral of General Luckin. At the time of his death, he was attached to the Pretoria Regiment and involved in the 'Defence Force Movement'. He was buried with full military honours and it is highly likely that his early demise was due to the injuries suffered on active service.

THE TALE BEHIND THE TALE

W.F.G. Thomas was my step-grandmother's first husband. Janet Dawson (chapter ten), as she was in 1917, had nursed him at some point during her wartime career, probably at Woking Military

Hospital. She moved to South Africa with him where they married and returned to England with her daughter after his death.

In 1967, on the day I went off to university to study history, Janet gave me a book about the exploits of the South African forces in France during the First World War. It was written by the famous fiction writer John Buchan. She told me that the book had belonged to her first husband who had been 'a South African war hero'. His name is written boldly on the flysheet in his own hand: 'Lieut W.F.G. Thomas M.C., 3rd Regt. South African Inf, Box 21, Randfontein.' Janet had also marked a couple of pages that would be of particular interest to me. At the time, the significance of her gift was completely lost on me in the excitement of leaving home. For years, the book remained one of a growing number of history books in my library and ignored as my personal historical interest lay elsewhere, mainly in the French Revolution of the eighteenth century.

When Janet died in the 1970s, I was already running a school history department and among the effects left to me was a box containing more of William Thomas's wartime memorabilia. This reminded me of the book which I'd then put in a safe place for future reference. I recovered the book and leafed through it, realising as I did (and to my shame) what I had missed in my youth. The marked pages were easy to find. Page 356 contained a note that 'Thomas, Second-Lieutenant W.F.G, infantry' was a recipient of the Military Cross. Pages 118 and 119 dealt with the action on the very first day of the Battle of Arras. At zero hour (5.30 a.m. on 9 April 1917):

> The 3rd Regiment, as it crossed the parapet and moved over No Man's Land, met with heavy machine-gun fire on its right flank, and suffered many casualties including Lieutenant Burrows killed, and Lieutenants Elliott, Money, Hyde, Gray, Thomas, Van Ryneveld, and Lee wounded.

This was the wound that led to his transfer to hospital in England, his meeting with his future wife and, in all probability, his death in the 1920s.

The other, more significant, reference was the easiest to find. Page 108 had been singled out with a heavily inked line down the side of the first paragraph and marked by a bundle of folded A4 sheets. I removed the sheets and read the marked paragraph:

> On January 3 1917, a party from the 3rd South African Regiment, commanded by Lieutenant B.W. Goodwin and W.F.G. Thomas made a successful raid on the German trenches. The men were picked volunteers who, for the week before, had been thoroughly trained in the work so that each knew exactly the task before him. All had blackened faces, and used only the Zulu language. After our barrage had drenched the enemy front line, the raiders entered the German trenches which were found to be very deep and magnificently constructed though badly damaged by our gunfire.

The passage also acknowledged the success of the raid (as quoted in the main tale above) while someone had later inserted into the text the letters 'M.C.' in ink behind the names of the two officers mentioned.

I was now more curious than a decade previously when first given the book and didn't immediately replace the folded page markers but opened them up to discover that they were the original orders for the successful trench raid. These included a last-minute handwritten letter from Lieutenant Colonel E.F. Thackeray C.M.G., D.S.O. According to a photograph opposite page 70 of the history book he was commander of the 3rd South African Regiment at the time. It was this letter and the accompanying raid orders that allowed me to tell Lieutenant Thomas's tale in detail. There are nine pages in all – in date order:

- Two pages – Top Secret typed order E.T. 101/3 dated 27/12/16 initialed E.T.
- Two-page handwritten letter by Thackeray ET 101/3 dated 29.12.16.
- Three pages marked Secret/The Officer Commanding 3rd S.A. Infantry handwritten Lt Thomas at top and Captain Pepper and signed by Capt. McDonald. 3rd page signed by Thackeray dated 30/12/16.
- Two-page Operation Order no 3 R/29 dated 1/1/17.

The orders are massively detailed and capable of commanding a lengthy article or booklet on their own. From them it becomes clear that the raid took place close to Claude Crater near Roclincourt just north of Arras. According to historians it was here that the concept of the trench or 'body snatcher' raid was first conjured up by the Canadians in September 1916, months

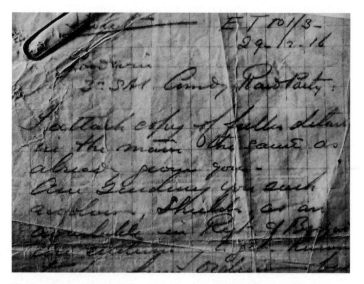

Handwritten trench raid orders from the commander of the 3rd SAI.

before the raid in which Lieutenant Thomas was involved. The handwritten note from Thackeray makes for a fascinating document. In it, the commander of the South African infantry writes that he is lending William Thomas his shield jacket as it would fit him but, for obvious reasons, William was instructed to remove Thackeray's name and rank from it! Thackeray ends his note with the encouraging comment, 'Let us know your wants – we will do all we can'.

The later details of Lieutenant Thomas's career were gleaned through the use of the ever-versatile search engine. 'W.F.G. Thomas M.C.' came up with references to Thomas's promotions and resignation towards the end of the war, flagged up in the digitised *London Gazette* as well as a version of Buchan's *History of the South African Forces in France* which is now available online. The memorabilia willed to me by my grandmother enabled me to flesh out the story. It included various obituaries, photographs of Lieutenant Thomas in his uniform, his two general service medals (the MC is apparently in a museum in South Africa) and a hymn sheet from the funeral of Sir Henry Timson Luckin KCB CMG DSO who had commanded the 9th Division in France. This took place in Pretoria in 1925 where there is a statue of Luckin. Handwritten notes on the hymn sheet suggest that 'Capt. Thomas M.C. and Mrs. Thomas SRN SGM' were both present at the funeral.

My step-grandmother spoke little about her first husband, although she was clearly proud of him. One obituary said: 'He was in every way an ideal soldier and won the respect, admiration and affection of all those with whom he was associated during the war.' The other noted that he was: 'A fine officer and a man of outstanding character.' Thanks to my step-grandmother's sense of worth, William's tale can now be told in full.

William Thomas MC (right) in uniform.

12

ERNEST BRIDGE (1896–1915) AND NORMAN BRIDGE (1897–1918): A TALE OF LOST BROTHERS

Ernest and Norman Bridge were brothers, the sons of Frederick James Bridge, a shopkeeper in the village of Roxwell near Chelmsford in Essex. Frederick was nick-named 'Bunny' Bridge because of protruding front teeth and seems to have been something of a local character. He was also an astute businessman. He invested money in stocks and shares and, according to passports which have been discovered during online research, travelled widely.

Ernest and Norman were the shopkeeper's only sons and, in early life, helped to run the shop which, like many similar businesses in the early twentieth century, was a hub of village life. Although situated only a few miles from the market town of Chelmsford, the shop was a successful enterprise. Few local folk, and especially farm labourers, had the wherewithal, the desire or the time to journey into town during the late Victorian and Edwardian periods. The Bridges were able to travel as they owned a horse and trap, which featured in many family photographs. One photograph that has survived shows the family outside the shop, the father and boys to the fore wearing their working white aprons. This photograph was featured in a parish calendar published in the late twentieth century.

During the war, Ernest served in the 7th Battalion of the Norfolk Regiment which was part of the 12th Eastern Division. He joined up at Norwich in 1914. At the time he was working for a baker in Much Hadham in Hertfordshire and was in training until called into action in May 1915 when the battalion moved across to join the 35th Brigade within the 12th Division. In July they were in the trenches in 'Plugstreet' (Ploegsteert) Woods. The woods lay in the southern part of the Ypres sector and formed part of a fairly quiet section of the front line where new troops were often blooded.

By the end of September, the battalion had moved nearer to Lille and was in and out of the front line for a few days while taking part in the early stages of the Battle of Loos. On 13 October, the 7th Norfolks were part of a mass attack on the German trenches. According to reports, this attack was thwarted by the accuracy of a single German machine-gunner. One hundred and sixty men were reported missing, Ernest among them. His body was never found. He was 19 years old.

Norman Bridge served in the 2nd Battalion of the Essex Regiment and enlisted at Chelmsford. He was in the services in April 1917 when he came home on leave and also spent some time, either in training or on standby, at Shoreham and at Halton Camp near Wendover. He also made a surprise visit home over the Christmas period of 1917. By April 1918, he was in France with his battalion which had become part of the

12th Brigade and 4th Division. The battalion was caught out by the German Spring Offensive and became involved in attritional hand-to-hand fighting in and around the village of Riez du Vinage between 18 and 21 April 1918. On 24 April, the battalion returned to its billets in Censé La Vallée and its officers were able to list and record casualties. There were forty-three killed, 115 wounded and thirty-six missing. Norman was never seen again. He was 20 years old.

Both of the Bridge boys are remembered on the Loos Memorial which contains the names of some 20,000 Allied officers and men with no known grave. Ernest's name is inscribed

Research Tip: Look out for the Machine-Gunner

The Lewis gun or Lewis Automatic Machine Gun was operated by 'machine-gunners'. The Germans had machine-gunners too and they were feared for both their tactical knowledge and accuracy. If your ancestor was a machine-gunner, then he was likely to be among the most hated group of men in the eyes of the opposition. Because of the nature of machine-gun fire, casualties in open battle were very high when machine guns were involved in an action. The Germans, for example, set up their crews at the corners of exposed fields and open land in order to catch anyone approaching in deadly crossfire. Thus it has been noted that machine-gunners were often singled out for summary execution if taken prisoner. As a result, the prospect of imprisonment by the enemy led those in machine-gun crews to remove anything from their clothing which indicated that they were involved in such activity.

on a memorial cross with two others close to St Andrew's Church, Northwold.

The village shop is still going in Roxwell. Today it is known as 'Deal's', as for many years in the early to middle of the twentieth century it was run by Billy Deal, who married one of Bunny Bridge's daughters. The way things worked in the twentieth century, if either of his sons had survived the First World War, it may have survived into the twenty-first century as 'Bridge's'. Such is the fickle finger of fate.

THE TALE BEHIND THE TALE

What follows (and in chapters thirteen and fourteen) is as much about the researcher and research techniques as it is about the subjects of the research. Ernest and Norman were my wife's great-uncles, brothers of her grandmother Grace Bridge. They both died some thirty to forty years before my wife's birth. I can recall my wartime great-uncles with clarity while family members of my wife's generation were not so fortunate. In this case and in those referred to in chapters thirteen and fourteen, the researcher was my wife's younger brother, Richard Monk, born in 1962. In the early part of the present century, he put together a large blue folder of family-related First World War material which he hopes will pass on down through the family. This is an admirable move and much of what follows is based on his researches.

In 2004 Richard, inspired by the 60th anniversary of D-Day and the fact that his father had recently retired from farming, made (in his own words): 'a day's trip to Belgium with my two sons age 13 and 10 to pay our respects to my grandmother's two brothers, who despite dying three years apart are both remembered on the same memorial at Loos.' At the time, Richard had gained all the initial information he needed from the War Graves Commission website but the visit only served to increase his curiosity. Although an agricultural economist by training, he has a deep love of history inherited from his mother and a researcher's skills gained as part of his university training. Again in his own words, the story he was then able to unravel came from: 'visits to the National Archives at Kew to see the War Diaries of the battalions in which my great-uncles served, the library at the Imperial War Museum and the Museum of the Essex Regiment in Chelmsford.' Most praiseworthy perhaps were his efforts to 'read a number of accounts of the Western Front to get a better understanding than I retained for my O-level history course'. This is to be highly recommended.

Richard's visit to the National Archives at Kew enabled him to narrow Ernest's last hours down to a specific attack on 13 October 1915 during the Battle of Loos. The account of this attack in the relevant war diary is quite detailed and refers to the inability of Mills bombers and earlier heavy bombardment to silence a single German machine-gunner who was responsible for many of the casualties. Richard notes that the outcome of the attack for the 7th Norfolks was: '66 other ranks killed, 196 wounded, 160 reported lost or missing with 3 officers killed and 7 wounded.' Ernest was one of the 'lost or missing'. As in many other cases, his main service record was destroyed in an air raid during the Second World War. Ernest's medal card, now available online, gives his service number, 14761, and notes that he entered the field of conflict on 30 May 1915. It also shows that he was awarded the two standard service medals plus the 1915 star and indicates the difficulties caused by the fog of war with the statement that he had died 'on or since 13/10/15'.

Norman's experiences during the war were less easy to piece together due to the missing records. Family memorabilia enabled Richard to follow Norman's movements prior to his appearance

Norman Bridge with two of his sisters.

at the front. The confusion over his final few days was established during Richard's visit to Kew where the war diary reports both British and German troops occupying houses in the village the 2nd Essex Regiment had been sent in to secure. Norman's sister Grace recorded her brother's death in her diary in May 1918. In September, the family received a confusing message which suggested that his body was buried near Merville. A month later, outstanding pay of 17s plus his Bible and flash lamp were sent home. In January 1920, the family received a final gratuity of £1 2s 6d. Norman's medal card shows that he was awarded the two standard service medals and that his service number was 202113.

Ernest is remembered on Panel 30 and 31 of the Loos Memorial and Norman on Panel 85 to 87. The Northwold War Memorial is flagged up on a couple of websites, one of which states that he is 'probably' the son of Frederick James Bridge and confirms the circumstances of his death. Such sites, detailing the information on war memorials then fleshing them out with further research, are both invaluable and growing. Some of them note that there are costs involved in setting up such sites and rightly request respect for their work and recognition from those who copy out their work, word-for-word and use it for personal gain.

Frederick J. Bridge, village shopkeeper, had two sons and four daughters born over a decade between 1895 and 1905. The daughters all lived to a ripe old age and I had the pleasure of coming in contact with them all in the late twentieth century.

13

FRED MONK: A TALE UNRAVELLED

Fred Monk was the son of a groom who worked on a large farm near the village of Good Easter in Essex. In the 1911 census, aged 13, he was described as a scholar. While still a teenager, he worked on a local farm. Fred went off to war late in the conflict, probably because his agricultural skills were needed at a time when there were concerns about food production. He arrived in France in 1917 and was stationed near a beach where he was saddled with the task of filling sandbags to be used in the trenches. Then one day and with little prior notice, he and his companions were taken off this task and put on a train. They arrived in Italy where they were marched through the country to show solidarity with the Italians. In time, they were back on a train heading for France and the front.

In the spring of 1918 when the German final push came, Fred was captured. He reckoned that he and his fellow captives were lucky. Their officers had been killed during the action, leaving the rest of the squad in a position to surrender. Once captive, he was fortunate enough to receive reasonable treatment. His captors discovered that he had worked with horses all his life and he was given the job of looking after horses in captivity. Despite this, like many other prisoners of war towards the end of the conflict, Fred suffered from a lack of nourishing food. He had to live off cabbage water for some time and his wife (he married after the conflict) reckoned that the experience in captivity affected him physically for life.

After the war his family found itself in a position to start farming on its own account and by the time of his death in 1979, Fred and his only son (my father-in-law) had built up a successful business in arable farming.

THE TALE BEHIND THE TALE

This case study is as much about process as it is about content. Fred Monk was the husband of Grace Bridge and the brother of Cyril Monk (chapter fourteen). He was also my wife's paternal grandfather. The tale as told above was just as the family was able to relate it during his lifetime. I first came across the family in 1971 and was told that Fred did not like to talk about his experiences in the war. Just before his death (and emboldened with party drink) I broached the subject with him, hoping to use his story in my school lessons. He repeated the story told by the family almost verbatim. When I asked him why he hadn't talked about it, he told me that he had 'never been asked'. Another lesson for us all!

After his grandfather's death and while putting together the stories of the members of the family who had lost their lives in the conflict, my wife's brother Richard (see chapter twelve) decided to see if he could find out more about Fred's experiences. Initial research led him to conclude that 'ironically, finding out about Fred was more difficult than the others because he lived'; another moot point. He discovered that Fred served in the 'Buffs' (specifically the 10th Battalion of the West Kent Regiment) and had been awarded the Victory Medal and British War Medal. He did not receive these until November 1922. As he had not been awarded the medals for earlier service, this was a good sign that he had joined up later in the war.

With the information gained on the Buffs, Richard then approached the regimental museum in Maidstone. At first, he drew a blank but somebody employed by the museum kindly kept up the sleuthing, and a few weeks after his initial request Richard was emailed a package of interesting information. (How often have we researchers benefited from the dedication and professionalism of such museum and library employees.) Frederick George (sometimes George Frederick), Monk G/21197 was reckoned to have joined the 10th Battalion of the Buffs 'around 4 May 1917'. According to the *Queen's Gazette*, a copy of which was held at the museum, he was reported missing in August 1918, confirmed as a prisoner of war in December 1918 and released in January 1919. The researcher also added, from personal knowledge, that Fred had probably been captured on 21 March 1918 at the very beginning of the German Spring Offensive: 'his battalion was overrun – even the commanding officer was captured'.

The information gained from the regimental museum encouraged Richard to take a trip to the National Archives at Kew to look up the battalion war diary. From this he established that during August and September 1917, the battalion was close to the Western Front 'near Bray and Zudcote' and in training for an advance 'along the Flanders' coast'. The training continued into October 1917 when there was a change of plan. The battalion (close to 1,000 men and officers in total) divided into two sections in the middle of November and headed by train for Italy. The record of activities there is very detailed and tells of long marches to reach the Italian Front, where they supported a battalion of the Queen's Regiment and a battalion of the Durham Light Infantry. There was little activity on this front

Research Tip: Get the Most out of the Web

When trying to find out as much as possible about named individuals I usually have the following five websites open; two pay sites, one free site and two search engines:

thegenealogist.co.uk
ancestry.co.uk
familysearch.org
google.co.uk
books.google.co.uk

The following First World War sites were either used or come recommended as well as sites for individual war, regimental and services' museums accessible through search engines:

forces-war-records.co.uk
nationalarchives.gov.uk/records/looking-for-person
1914-1918.net
ww1battlefields.co.uk
wartimememoriesproject.com/greatwar
scarletfinders.co.uk/8.html
london-gazette.co.uk
tunnellersmemorial.com
1914-1918.invisionzone.com/forums/index php?act=idx
westernfrontassociation.com

although there were occasional casualties and some men were evacuated from the trenches as the snow and ice began to bite in December. At times the battalion was kept in reserve when it seemed to practise a great deal of marching. It was back on the Italian Front in late February, where some contact was made with the enemy.

Early in March 1918 the battalion was taken by bus to Padua from where it returned to France by train. Additions were made to the battalion so, in theory, it had about 1,000 men in a position to fight; in fact there were nearly 700 officers and men moved to Fremicourt on 22 March and overnight on to Morchies where it took a defensive position at 3 a.m. By the evening the battalion had been outflanked by the Germans and only 120 returned to base. Most of the men were posted missing and, as it later turned out, had been captured, Fred among them. As he concluded these particular researches Richard remarked that he had also been informed that 'the understanding is that he [Fred] was not demobilised until quite late due to his poor state of health in captivity'.

In 2006, Richard paid the CICR (International Red Cross in Geneva) for two hours' research and as a result received a stamped attestation that Frederick Monk, a private in the 10th R.W. Kent Regiment, 'born Essex 21.04.1897, no. 21197 had been captured '23.03.1918 place unstated' and that the place of internment was 'in Parchim Lager [Mecklenburg] coming from western front'. This information had been logged on 4 July 1918. In terms of repatriation, he 'arrived at Dover on 30.11.1918 and retrained for Canterbury' (according to an undated list). The Red Cross had gleaned this information from one list coming from German authorities and one from the British.

So Fred's tale had been fleshed out by the time the current book came to be written. The question remained: was the internet able to come up with any more detail gathered in recent years?

Fred Monk in uniform.

The answer is a resounding 'Yes'. In the first instance, there has been much online discussion concerning the POW camp at Parchim. One researcher whose ancestor had been in the camp noted that the soldier's experiences as a POW had turned his dark hair white and that 'his physical state was such that he was virtually unrecognisable to his family when he came home'. Another suggested that the camp housed prisoners from at least eight nations. A third argued that Parchim was just a registration camp and that prisoners were moved on to work camps which were not examined by the Red Cross, which might explain the poor condition in which many returned home. Finally, a contributor noted that his ancestor had spent considerable time in hospital after repatriation 'like several thousand others. It is impossible to gauge what these chaps went through'.

'God rest them all,' he concluded.

By this point, Fred's tale as told by himself and his family had been filled out and all seemed to back up what he had said. Compared with some of the other case studies researched for this book there still remained gaps, so it was with extreme joy that I then discovered that his 'short service' record had survived and could be examined online. (As noted above relatively few short service records have survived.) This record showed that he enlisted into the 4th Battalion of the Buffs (No. 6147). His address was Fouchers' Farm, Good Easter and he was a farm hand employed by the Lodge family at nearby Roxwell. He was 18 years and 8 months at the time and had signed on at Chelmsford in Essex and was 5ft 6½in tall. Although he was 'attested' on 11 December 1915 as a private, he was placed in the reserves a month later and not mobilised until 22 January 1917. (Initially an Army Form B had exempted him for service up to 31 August 1916.) From January up to 22 September 1917, his service was all in England. In July 1917, he sprained his ankle while on operations with the battalion at Barham and had to spend some time in hospital. This was followed by a bout of tonsillitis. He arrived at the infamous 38 base at Étaples on 24 September 1917. All in all his service record had him spending twenty-one months in England (which must have included his time on standby) followed by three months in France, four months in Italy and eight months as a prisoner of war. On demobilisation in February 1919, he was placed into class Z. This meant that he could be recalled to the army if there were problems during the peace negotiations. At times in this record, he was described as a 'horse-man', which is interesting in light of the recent success of the stage show and feature film *War Horse*. He was awarded the two usual service medals.

Fred Monk's story is a fine example of a countryman at war. Were he still around today, we might have been able to prompt his memory even further with the information recently gathered.

14

CYRIL MONK (1899–1917):
THE TALE OF A PRECIOUS SON

Cyril Bohannon Monk was the son of James Monk, a groom to an Essex landowning and farming family just outside of Chelmsford near the village of Good Easter. He was also the younger brother of Fred Monk (chapter thirteen). At the age of 11 he was recorded as a 'scholar' and a typed letter dated February 1913 shows that he was working in an office, could type and was learning shorthand at the age of 13.

When he joined up in 1917, Cyril was working in a solicitor's office in Chelmsford. He enlisted as a private in the 10th Battalion of the Essex Regiment and, according to entries in the *Essex Chronicle*, was wounded twice in 1917: in May and later in November. On the first occasion, the battalion was operating around Heininel on the Hindenburg Line; on the second it was stationed in the Houthurst Forest at Louvois Farm.

In July 1918, the same *Chronicle* reported Cyril as 'posted missing', although the War Graves Commission records his death as 26 April 1918 during the infamous German Spring Offensive. In their 1926 work 'With the 10th Essex in France' authors Banks and Chell record that in April 1918 the battalion was involved in activities in Hangard Wood on the Somme. It was ordered to attack the wood early in the evening of 25 April and there was much confusion as neighbouring Allied troops were trying to occupy the same ground at the same time. All this was happening under heavy shellfire.

At dawn on 26 April, the battalion was dug in in the middle of the wood and ready for a new attack. Visibility was poor and there was little in the way of preparatory shelling. As the men moved forward, they were greeted by a nest of German machine guns. There was considerable confusion in the British ranks as different units intermingled and many officers were lost.

On the morning of 27 April, the battalion was relieved by the French and the frightening extent of casualties was revealed. It had lost twelve officers and 201 other ranks. There were only sixty to seventy men and four officers left standing. Cyril was reported missing during this battle and was never seen again. His name appears on Panels 51 and 52 of the Pozières Memorial near Albert, some 20km north of Hangard. His is also one of thirteen names recorded on the war memorial in St Andrew's church graveyard, Good Easter. The accompanying note on the memorial's website reads:

Cyril B. Monk (poss. MONK, CYRIL BOHANNON)
Private. 10thBn. EssexRegiment.
Died 26/04/1918.
Service no. 42960.
Pozières Memorial, France.

THE TALE BEHIND THE TALE

Cyril Monk was the youngest in the family and the apple of his mother's eye. His future lay in the town not in the country and as a young teenager he was already making progress. Letters held by the family show him to have been a bright and intelligent youngster. His ability to type and willingness to learn shorthand at the age of 13 have already been mentioned. His natural talent is obvious from letters written to his brother Leonard in March 1918 when he had just moved from Colchester to Norwich:

Am billeted with two pals with a Mrs. Coleman. They have two children at home and one in the army. The two at home are girls (11 and 13 respectively). Could not be more comfortable in a billet.

He also seems to have been a capable musician:

There is a piano in the billet at my disposal for playing and you can guess this suits me. It is a fine instrument in both tone and touch – an upright grand.

When he wrote this letter he headed it L/C C B Monk 10912 B Company 52 (Trad) Bedfords. This is rather confusing as less than a month later he was recorded as being killed while serving with the Essex Regiment. It seems pretty certain that he was with the Bedfords in England just prior to his death. The history of the battalion to which the Bedfords were attached notes that they trained at Colchester before moving to Norwich in February 1918. This fits in with Cecil's letter writing. The battalion was also noted as having 'no regimental affiliation' which may explain his eventual movement to the Essex Regiment.

Although movement from regiment to regiment at short notice seems to have been a regular occurrence, particularly

Plaque commemorating Cyril Monk.

Cyril Monk in uniform.

during the later years of the war, the story of Cyril's death remained riddled with doubt for some time. The family story has it that Cyril was considered 'missing' for years after. He was said to have disappeared in mysterious circumstances and his mother expected him to walk through the door at any time. Interestingly the notes on the local war memorial website also express a slight doubt as to the true story behind 'C.B. Monk' and this despite the fact that the family had been forwarded Cyril's 'fallen for King and Country' plaque.

There is a photograph of Cyril in uniform which accents his youth and reminds one of the sacrifice of youth made in the war.

Research Tip: Look out for the 'Dead Man's Penny'.

The first time you come across a memorial death plaque from the First World War, it comes as something of a shock; it is so much bigger than the medals awarded for service and bravery. The plaque gained its macabre nickname for an obvious reason. The person named on it had to be dead in order to have it sent to his next of kin. Between 1.25 million and 1.5 million of the plaques were produced and covered deaths in service from the outbreak of war in August 1914 right through to April 1920, some eighteen months after the cessation of hostilities. The plaques have the names of the victims alone without reference to rank or regiment and a small number relate to females. Today blank plaques can still be obtained if descendants are interested in recreating some form of personal memorial. The next of kin may also have received separately a letter from the victim's commanding officer and/or a scroll.

15

FREDERICK JAMES SLEATH:
THE TALE OF A SNIPER OFFICER

Fred Sleath was a young Scot. He was in his mid-20s when promoted to second lieutenant in the Royal Scots in 1915. As an officer he served on the Western Front and was heavily involved in organising sniping in and around Ypres. Later in the war, he was transferred to military intelligence and was given the task of interviewing wounded soldiers when they returned home from the front. During his time in military intelligence he jotted down some of his observations on the art of sniping based on his experiences earlier in the conflict, seemingly with the intentions of publishing a book.

According to Fred, although life on the front was dangerous for everyone, snipers were particularly in the firing line:

At night, you may be walking along a road just behind the firing line. All of a sudden something whoops past your ear; you see a momentary flash of light and get a sensation of tremendous force like an express train rushing past. It is only some time afterwards when your scattered senses have collected themselves that you realise that a bullet has missed your head by the barest fraction. During night watch, you may be standing on the fire-step beside a sentry looking out towards the German lines. In front of you, an occasional rifle is flashing as a German sentry fires blindly into the shadows. On either side of you, British sentries are doing the same thing. Then the sandbag, which your chin is touching, seems as if struck by a mighty hammer and your eyes are blinded by flying soil. You stumble down in the trench and, though you know you are not hurt, you feel certain that your companion has been hit. You turn to find him gazing at you, mutely express-ing the same idea about yourself. A random bullet has struck the sandbag between you.

Such incidents will be recognised by every man in the trench area. You cannot see them, nor can you prevent them. The bullet comes out of the night. You do not see it come. The danger is over before you realise its presence and you ascribe your escape to pure chance.

Our snipers naturally experience more of such incidents than the ordinary soldier.

In such circumstances, snipers had to take extra special care:

It is not only in times of crisis that an instinct asserts itself; it appears continually in the ordinary trench routine from day to day. Experienced snipers for example never leave their loophole without closing the protecting panel. Many men have been killed by a bullet coming through a loophole left carelessly unguarded. At the same time, if you speak to a sniper engaged in observation work, though he may turn to you with the dazed entranced look of a man interrupted in a pursuit into which he is throwing his whole energy, you will see his hand steal up mechanically to the handle of the protecting plate and swing the panel back into place.

In some parts of the trenches, snipers will walk confidently with heads erect but in other parts they are obviously ill at ease and often will shamelessly adopt a crouching position. It is safe to assume that here the trench wall is insecure.

Time and again has the sniper's instinct warned him aright and whole sections of the trench have been rebuilt because the parapet was not bullet proof – though, to outward appearance, it seemed to afford serviceable protection.

On one occasion in a well-known and dangerous area of the front, a sniping unit was on patrol in search of a new base from which to attack the enemy:

A few yards behind our firing line in the Ypres-Messines sector, there was an old house at the side of the main communication trench. Although German shells had piled the roof down in ruins onto the remains of the second floor, enough of the house had been left to give a very good view of the German trenches. Here a sniping officer decided to build a post for sniping and observation. Taking up the whole of a single night, he and a party of his men laboured strenuously at the project and, while making as little change as possible in the existing structure, by judicious rearrangement of the roof beams created a space where a sniper could comfortably command the German line and yet remain completely hidden from enemy observation. The post could not be rendered bullet proof – only cover from view could be afforded and easy access was gained by means of a ladder placed against the rear wall which was itself broad enough to act as an effective screen.

In the early grey of the morning, the sniper officer stood in front of the house and examined their handiwork. A sniper was already at the post and, short as the intervening distance was, the officer could not detect his presence nor could he see anything to indicate the changes, which had been made. Up to now, however, the opposing German snipers had proved themselves a very efficient set of fellows and not the slightest precaution could be overlooked in dealing with them.

Although he could not find a single point, which would give away the post to the Germans, the officer was still not satisfied and finally ordered the sniper to come down.

'We will see what happens during the day before we use it', was the explanation he gave to his men – and they were content.

A fox will desert its hole in the earth and seek new quarters the day before the farmer comes to dig him out. Why it acts so, the fox does not understand nor was the sniper officer in a better position regarding his action. In both cases, the actions were justified by results. For the whole of that day, the officer stood with his men and watched the newly created position being cut to pieces by the concentrated fire of several German snipers who, whether by chance or by skill, had located the post within an hour of dawn.

One sniper, something of a villain before the war, had fallen out with his father yet was able to reveal another side to his personality in conversation with his officer:

The sniper had plans for developing his father's business after the war and it was clear to the officer that, despite all that had gone before, Charlie still held his father in high esteem.

This observation was to find further significance on a certain misty day when Charlie and his officer were observing the German lines from one of the sniping posts. Through his high power periscope, the officer saw an old German Landsturmer, evidently a straggler from a night working party; he appeared round the edge of a broken down farmhouse behind the German trenches. He looked so utterly miserable that the officer hesitated to indicate him to the sniper but Charlie has seen him, his rifle cracked and the German disappeared out of sight.

'I've shot an old man,' he said.

Then, after a pause, he added,

'He was awful like my feyther.'

There were tears in Charlie's eyes and his lips twitched curiously. With a sinking heart, the officer instinctively divined that the improvement of the last few weeks threatened to come undone.

'He would not have looked like your "feyther" had he got you in the line of his sights,' the officer noted almost brutally as he tried to change the bent of the boy's thoughts but Charlie did not seem to hear. The old imbecilic look had come back into his eyes and all that day he mooned around the trench, leaving his observer to work alone.

The officer, being a decent sort, detailed one of the other snipers to keep Charlie unobtrusively under observation.

The relapse was not, thankfully, of long duration. That evening, Charlie, another sniper and the officer stood on the firing step, looking out towards the enemy trenches. The light was poor and it seemed impossible that the Germans could see them – but it is just at such moments of relaxed watchfulness that death comes searching and swooping across the open. A rifle cracked from the German lines and the other sniper slid to the bottom of the trench with a hole in his head the size of a man's fist.

A wound as ghastly as this could only be caused by a bullet which had been tampered with (the sort which German snipers sometimes use) and the grief of the dead sniper's comrades was made even sharper by resentment.

'I'm awful glad I shot that old man this morning,' Charlie said quietly, the manic look no longer in his eyes.

Thenceforth, he went about his work with greater determination and energy than before.

Snipers came from all walks of life:

The sniper-sergeant of a certain territorial regiment had been a Divinity student before the war and in the cloisters of a stately university he had dreamed his dreams and wrestled in an academic way with the problems of the end-all and be-all of existence. The call to duty brought him face to face with the actualities of life and death. As one result of his university training, he wrote beautiful notes on such points as the proper placing in the parapet of steel loophole plates. When death claimed him, his successor fell heir to the manuscript text book, in which was treated in scholarly fashion every aspect of the sniper's art.

A sniper's loophole near Ypres.

And a final tale brings out the human side of life in the trenches. On one occasion, a group of snipers had set themselves up only 20yd from an enemy outpost:

> Suddenly out of the darkness loomed a bulky figure in the German uniform and a voice speaking in perfect English bade them 'Good Evening'. He had not come with any hostile intentions, nor yet to give himself up as a prisoner. He had come to talk the language and speak with the men of the country, which had fed and sheltered him for many years. There crouched together between the hostile lines, Germans and Britons sat and talked. He told them of the unpopularity of the war with his comrades and himself and of their hardships; he spoke of his life in England and finally he asked for some bully beef as he and his comrades in the bombing post were very hungry. Presently with every expression of friendliness the strange acquaintances parted.

THE TALE BEHIND THE TALE

Fred Sleath's tale can be told as a result of a chance discovery in the attic of a 'White Elephant' shop in Carlisle in the 1980s. My father, who had an interest in ephemera, was asked to clear out the contents of the attic and he passed on a number of things to me which he thought might be of interest and use in my teaching of history to teenagers (see next chapter too). Among these was a manuscript bound in brown paper mostly typed but some of it handwritten. The title of the manuscript is *The British Sniper* and it is divided into twenty-six 'articles' or chapters averaging some 2,000 to 3,000 words each. An initial reading of the text revealed that it was written around 1917 and based on the author's experiences as an intelligence officer in charge of sniping over a large section of the Western Front around Ypres

3.

as part of / our military establishment , nevertheless we were far from being devoid of means to cope with the activities of these fellows .   The insistence by the army authorities on certain standards of markmanship , and their fostering of special excellence by providing efficiency tests bringing extra pay to those who passed them, combined with their wise encouragement of rifle-meetings where army shots acquired experience in competitive shooting against the best shots of the empire, had developed a high standard of efficiency in the use of the rifle throughout the British army , and from this general excellence had evolved a large number of really good marksman,whose skill was at least equal to anything the German Jaegers could achieve.

It was these *devoted men who on their own* initiative put up the first resistance of the British army to the German sniper , spending the little leisure which the arduous trench labour left tothem in trying to silence some German sharpshooter , whose constant sniping was sorely harassing their comrades.   Thus each regiment gradually became possessed of a volunteer sniping section , which formed a splendid nucleus for the later organisations , and though not officially recognised , it was pretty generally understood that the men composing these sections were free to devote as much of their time as they liked to sniping.

How typical this is of Britain in all her varied activities !   First comes the pioneers pressing out into the unknown, through danger and suffering and deathx , until success crowns their efforts.   And along the path which they have blazed , and towards the goal which their voluntary efforts have made assured , travels British authorities with its symbols of organisation and government

An extract from the original text for the sniper's book.

Research Tip: Read Around the Subject

Good advice given me by my history tutor. Here are ten books/series of books from my own First World War library:

The War Illustrated; A pictorial record of the conflict of nations, J.A.Hammerton (ed.), The Amalgamated Press (numerous bound volumes – issued as separate magazines during the war, August 1914–September 1919).

The History of the Great War, Newman Fowler (ed.), (Waverley Book Co., 6 volumes, 1919).

A Popular History of the Great War, J.A. Hammerton (Fleetway House, 6 volumes, 1933).

Battleground Europe: Hill 60 Ypres, Nigel Cave (Leo Cooper, 2004).

Tracing Your First World War Ancestors, Simon Fowler (Countryside Books, 2003).

Gallipoli, L.A. Carlyon (Bantam Books, 2003).

The Bells of Hell Go Ting-a-ling-a-ling, Eric Hiscock (Corgi, 1977).

The Rhymes of a Red Cross Man, Robert Service (Ernest Benn Ltd, 1929).

In Flanders Field, Leon Wolff (Penguin Books, 1979).

Echoes of the Great War: The Diary of the Reverend Andrew Clark 1914 -1919, James Munson (ed.) (OUP, 1985).

between 1915 and 1916. It is felt with some certainty that the author was the father of the previous owner of the shop and his name and position were neatly written inside the cover:

Fred J Sleath 2/Lieut
Sutherland House
1, Norfolk Square
Paddington
W2

The manuscript also had two other helpful pieces of memorabilia inside. One was a card with a string tie on it indicating that it had once been attached to some kind of attaché case. It was dated 15 April 1917, marked OHMS and stamped by the Embarkation Commandant Southampton. This 'pass' allowed Lieutenant Sleath (by now MI W O – Military Intelligence, War Office), access to any dock. The other, a letter dated 15 April 1917 from the Surgeon General at the War Office, gave Sleath permission to interview wounded men just back from the fighting in France as part of Military Intelligence.

Fred Sleath's booklet proved to be such an interesting and informative primary source that it became important to know a little more about him and the usual sources for gathering information about a First World War combatant provided very helpful evidence. A medal roll card at the National Archives shows that he was a second lieutenant in the Royal Scots and had earned the right to the two general medals as well as the 1915 star. The same card came up with a home address in Bo'ness, Linlithgow, Scotland. Fortunately, Bo'ness appears to have been the family home in both 1891 and 1901 and these censuses show Frederick James Sleath there as the son of a Presbyterian minister, born in 1888.

Proving the point that general search engines such as Google should always be consulted and often come up with vital evidence, such a general search found a reference to Fred in a digitised version of the *London Gazette* for 10 March 1915 upon his temporary appointment as a second lieutenant. Fred's appointment as an officer may prove important in dating the start of his work as a sniping officer. His father Samuel also turned up as the result of a similar search – an English-born minister who held a significant Church office in Scotland.

Though written in the third person, the stories in the manuscript are clearly drawn from first-hand experience and 'the officer' appearing in various tales is likely to have been Fred himself. The opening chapter deals with all the general aspects of sniping in the First World War: a description of the British sniper, rivalry with German snipers, the formation of sniping units, areas of pre-war expertise of snipers and the role of intelligence officer. It also deals with the importance of the sniper's role, especially in holding up the German advance. The main text draws on hundreds of examples of sniping life with headings including: 'Night patrols', 'Super snipers', 'The Intelligence Officer', 'A sniper's grave' and 'Scotching a sniper's nest'. One particularly powerful chapter entitled 'Sniper Brown' is dedicated to the life and operations of a single sniper.

It is impossible to read Lieutenant Sleath's work without being impressed with the power of his description, which begs the question – was the manuscript ever published? A general internet research reveals that Fred Sleath survived the war to become a writer. An account of a gathering in Bo'ness in the 1920s runs:

> Perhaps some of the grownups read copies of Fred Sleath's newly published book, 'Breaker of Ships'. Unlike his two earlier successful works which were both thrillers, this was a novel set in "a small Scottish seaport town", and for Bo'nessians there was the

added interest of trying to identify their friends and neighbours among the characters.

Intriguingly, internet book sites reveal that in 1919, Fred Sleath produced a 'first novel' entitled *Sniper Jackson* which was digitised in 2010 by a firm called Bibliobazaar.

Unlike 'sappers' snipers did not have their 'positions' placed on official record. Nevertheless, tales of 'snipers' in the family continue to be passed down as was the case with John Stephens (chapter two) where the family still has one of his target practice books.

Fred Sleath's death is recorded in Durham towards the end of 1966.

16

REGINALD BANYARD:
A TRULY REMARKABLE TALE

Reginald Banyard, born 1895, was the son of a Cambridgeshire bricklayer. Like Cyril Monk (chapter fourteen), he must have been a bright lad, as by the age of 15 he was working as a solicitor's clerk. He was also looking after his widowed mother. He joined the army at Wisbech in May 1915 when one month short of his 20th birthday and became Sapper Banyard (84394) as part of the 203rd Royal Engineers Field Company. The field company had been formed early in 1915 and in July of that year moved up to Fearby in Yorkshire before spending time in training near Swindon and Tidworth.

The company left Southampton at the end of January and by the end of February was at the front and tasked with the job of draining trenches. The men were also inspected by Kitchener on 11 February. Reg seems to have been involved in this kind of desultory work, with the occasional scare from an enemy aeroplane and shelling right up to the beginning of the Somme campaign at the end of June. During this period he celebrated his twenty-first birthday.

Reg and the rest of the company came into the Somme arena on 9 July 1916, when they arrived at the village of Harponville near Albert. He was billeted for the night with Mr Decroix the baker. In the evening he went for a walk with the baker's daughter Lucille and, on his own admission, they 'fell in love'. On the following day, the battalion moved on the Albert itself and over the next few weeks was in the thick of the action around Morlancourt. The men moved regularly between the R.E. dump and the front, building and repairing. Reg saw people on guard duty killed and the battalion was shelled one day while on parade. The places where they were working were given names such as Happy Valley, Hell's Gate and Death Vale. One of the casualties during this period was a friend called Joe Skipper who was wounded and died a few days later.

On 3 August 1916 Reg had a few days respite so he took a cycle and headed back to Harponville to see Lucille. The only military person there was the padre who gave Reg the bad news that there had been an attack on the village on 13 July and that Lucille and her parents had been killed.

The remainder of August was spent around Carnoy, Happy Valley and a place known as The Citadel with the battalion involved in constructing new dugouts. Reg was in and out of the front line for the next few months and spent Christmas Day at the front. On the last day of the year, he contracted flu and spent a week in hospital. On release, he worked in an office for the remainder of January while his colleagues, now away from the front, converted local barns into billets for resting soldiers.

By February 1917, Reg was back in hospital again, this time with a severe cold. By the time of his release from hospital, his battalion was off to Wiencourt Camp. From here they were working between the R.E. 'dump' and the front line, guided forward and backwards by a French guide. Reg became so frustrated with the incompetence of the guide that he threatened to shoot him and eventually reported him to officers as a possible saboteur.

In March 1917, the battalion was involved in building dugouts again and Reg was once more confined to bed for a few days, this time on the orders of an officer, 'Mr Laidlaw'. On his return he and his companions were moving steadily forwards through the old German front line. In June 1917, after another short spell in hospital, he was recommended for a Distinguished Conduct Medal and promotion and sent home on leave. After training under commission, he returned to France and the thick of the action in August 1917. By now he was among the Highland Light Infantry (HLI) and Durham Light Infantry (DLI), whizz bangs and shells, and mid-August was taken up with attack and counter attack. At one point in the confusion of action, he was nearly arrested by an artillery officer as a spy.

On 25 August 1917, Reg 'got a dose of gas' while laying cables in the trenches. He returned to his work the following day but by early September was so 'sick' and 'queer' that he could not continue. He sought out a doctor who ordered him to Casualty Clearing Station 21 at Tincourt. His eyes were worsening and he was unable to see so he was transferred by train to 29 General Hospital at Rouen and thence by HMHS *Australia* back to England.

By mid-October 1917, Reg was being treated in the County Hospital at Winchester and as the month progressed began to be taken out for pub trips and home visits by members of the local aristocracy – namely a Lady Portal and a Lady Johnson. At one point he was recuperating at her home – Marsh Court House. Progress was slow and by Christmas he was still very ill and unsteady and was transferred nearer to home and No. 1 E G Hospital in Cambridgeshire.

This proved to be the end of his war.

THE TALE BEHIND THE TALE

Reg Banyard's remarkably full tale can be told as a result of material discovered in the same 'White Elephant' shop clear-out as that mentioned in Fred Sleath's tale (chapter fifteen). I can also recall my father suggesting that the two tales were linked by marriage and it is most likely that Fred Sleath's son married Reg Banyard's daughter. My mother met Reg on a number of occasions in later life and says that he was a charming and pleasant man.

Reg's tale is mainly based on information contained in two little pocketbooks, the latter of the two being a diary for 1917 and the first a fascinating little flip-over black book held together by an elastic band. This pocketbook is close to commanding the prize for the most intriguing piece of evidence I came across while writing the book. It was used for everything from noting names and addresses, wiring diagrams and details of evidence collected on sorties into no-man's-land to a journal of daily events. He started the journal part of the book on the day he embarked from Southampton and it runs into 1917 when it was overtaken by the diary.

The story of his brief 'love affair' (if it could even be called that) would move the hardest of hearts, especially as it had to be pieced together from different entries in the book. The account of his billeting with Decroix the baker and meeting Lucille is told twice in different parts of the journal side of the diary. The fact that they 'fell in love' is marked with an asterisk. His return to the village and discovery of the deaths of the family appears later in the journal. Most moving of all is a handwritten note in French signed and dated by Lucille herself, in the circumstances a stunningly moving reminder of the tragedy of war. The note was written out in what appears to be a form of vernacular French or even with a key word missing. The drift appears to be

The poem written by Lucille days before her death by shelling.

that Reg should live his life to the full. God had finished some of his work on the world but had left some for Reg to finish too:

Vivez chaque jour a votre tres mielleur. Le travail du mond est fini par peu de Dieu demande que un petit peu est fini par vous.

One or two of the addresses have been entered in the book in other hands but the most interesting, not to say unusual, 'foreign' entry runs:

Should the war end by the end of October 1916 I will pay to the Red Cross Society (Cambs) the sum of two pounds sterling (£2)

Signed A.E. Titchmarsh – witnessed by Banyard and another [indecipherable]

> ### Research Tip: Split Your Infinitives 'to Boldly Go' with Online Search Engines.
>
> To some it may be self-evident yet it remains important enough to affirm – online search engines such as Google are to be treasured. In many ways lists of books, booklets and online sites we associate with the back of research books are no longer necessary as it is more than likely that the first page thrown up by a good search engine will lead a researcher to a helpful book or site. The precision of that information can depend on the words placed initially in the search box and the way in which they are placed i.e. 'Reg Banyard' and 'Royal Engineers' is likely to be more successful than Reg Banyard Royal Engineers. Experimentation can also be helpful as in 'Reginald Banyard R.E.' or simply 'R. Banyard'. Persistence is also advisable. Other key words might be thrown in such as 'Cambridge', 'silver badge' or 'Western Front', which might lead to a site where another researcher has shown interest in the same person. The engines are particularly useful when building up background information and in this particular book they led to details on field hospitals, war diaries and war memorials.

Alan Edward Titchmarsh appears, from further sleuthing, to have been a sapper in the same battalion as Reg Banyard although he later joined the RAF. After the war, he worked for the Cambridge University Press. (Despite his unusual name, he does not appear to be directly related to the famous gardener and writer of the same name.) The black book entry indicates that Reg and Alan, presumably like many of their colleagues on the front, had differing opinions about when the war was going to come to an end.

A small photograph of Reg Banyard.

In the black book there is also a record of the watch Reg wore (a Climax watch, registration No. 529337) plus scribbled notes and diagrams for setting up an advanced post with wire and machine gun. There are also wiring diagrams including one for a Morse-code tapper and a handwritten Morse alphabet. In addition, a poem entitled 'Keep Smiling' was written up in the book. According to online sources, it appeared in print in *The Observer* on 13 October 1917 under the initials 'ECH Trenches France' and had been recovered from its initial publication in *Premier* magazine. It reads like a real morale booster. Under the front cover, there was a small loose photograph of Reg Banyard himself.

Thanks to this pocketbook, it is also possible to follow Reg on a foray across the front line and into no-man's-land in order to check work that needed to be done. The party was under the command of a Lieutenant Meadows and if the company diary is right, the area covered is Trones Wood. Here are some extracts from the notes taken by Reg (although it is not clear whether the trenches being examined are Allied or captured enemy ones):

Lt Meadows Recon 10/8/16

- Fill in one trench
- Line broken very much
- Mined tunnel
- Small trench filling 1'6" wide by 2'6"
- Slight declivity at edge of wood may be filled in

Northern Track

- Barbed wire
- 6 tree stumps to be removed
- Road broken and trees lying around

- Clear bank and hedgerow incline
- Remove bank of sunken road
- Lots of dead along sunken road
- NB trench behind wood very wide (left) and abundance of tools in trench to the right

Research Tip: Think about the Reliability of Certain Sources

One reason for putting Reg Banyard's pocketbook high on my list of useful sources is that it is filled with random, sometime unconscious, scraps of evidence. This leaves readers able to build up a picture of what happened themselves and allows them to draw their own conclusions. Sometimes diary or letter writers set out to write at length with an objective in mind and such writing needs to be approached with caution. In the 'Tale Behind the Tale' accompanying Fred Stephens's tale (chapter one), the story of the letter and the diary written by the same author and telling different stories was discussed. This is a case in point. In addition, Fred said that he transcribed his diaries faithfully into an exercise book in 1919 before the originals fell to pieces. One wonders whether this transcription was truly 'word for word'. Would he not have been inclined to change bits of text here and there on reflection now that he was far away from the heat of action? In general most of the primary material used in the book seems to be fairly reliable. War, however, does throw up a great deal of bias and propaganda and this has to be treated with due respect if the aim of the research is to get as near to the truth as possible.

All of this is also useful in working out the type of daily work carried out on the front by sappers.

Given the compelling nature of Reg Banyard's tale as it could be unravelled from the two books alone, the survival of many of his war records comes as a real bonus, enabling a fuller analysis of what happened to him (in particular after his diary ends in December 1917). Included in these are a silver badge record, a pension record and a medal roll card, all three digitised and available online on the *Ancestry* site.

The silver badge was worn by those who had been in the armed forces and could no longer serve because of injury or illness. It was awarded so the bearer would not be stopped in the street and accused of cowardice or, as in the case of certain young men known to one of the sisters of the Bridge boys (chapter twelve), given white feathers. The badge was also a mark of honour. The words 'For King and Empire' and 'Services Rendered' were marked on it. As the writer of the notes on the *Ancestry* site notes, nearly three quarters of a million Empire service personnel were killed in the war and 'an even greater number were discharged because of wounds or illness'. In Reg Banyard's case (84394 of the Royal Engineers 3rd reserve battalion), he was awarded badge No. 361429 on 10 May 1918 at the age of 23. The reason for his discharge was given as 'gas poisoning'. As the diary ended in December 1917, this is a useful indicator that he failed to recover fully over the following few months.

There are five documents in Reg's online pension record. The first is his short service attestation signed when he joined up in 1915 giving details of his age, address, occupation and the fact that he signed up with the Royal Engineers at Wisbech. On the second sheet, information has been stored later in a haphazard fashion. Under the marital heading is a typed note stating that he did not have to attend for examination (according to a 1917 regulation). Under details of 'children' is his record broken down viz:

'service at home from 10.5.15 to 27.1.16 then B.E.F from 28.1.16 to 17?8.17 then Home from 11.10.17 to 10.5.18.' On the same sheet under 'Statement of Services' are initialled details of his attestation in 1915, embarkation in 1916 and his eventual discharge as no longer fit for military service in 1918. His pensionable service was calculated to be three years and one month.

The next document is a medical report from the Eastern General Hospital (Army Form B179) dated 28 April 1918. It gives the date of the 'injury' ('he says 10 September 1917') at Ronsay. It is noted that he went back into action but fainted several times and was short of breath. 'Gas poisoning on active service' was the ultimate conclusion. The next sheet includes indecipherable medical notes which indicate that he 'looked well' but may have had problems with his blood count and that he was considered unsuitable for military service. The final sheet suggests that he should be examined in three months' time and that, for pensionable purposes, no permanent disability was anticipated.

His medal roll card is, like many others, concise but informative. He received his two service medals (and apparently no DCM or commission) and his award of the silver badge is also noted as is his date of enlistment and date of discharge, three years and three days later.

Also online is the diary of his battalion and considerable detail of its role, all of which adds to the telling of the tale. An admirable online 'short history' of the company shows that Lieutenant Meadows of the reconnaissance mission was in charge of number 4 section. The unfortunate Lieutenant Laidlaw who sent Reg to bed was injured in 1916 and later killed by a stray shell after Reg's departure from France. Further online sleuthing also led to more on his companion 'Joe Skipper', whose injury and eventual death on the Somme Reg recorded in his black book. According to the War Graves Commission, Joseph Allen Skipper, born *c.* 1893, died on 27 July 1916 and is buried at Boulogne.

His parents were Harry and Annie, and at the time of the 1911 census Joe, age 17, had been living in Stapleford in Nottinghamshire and working as an early motor engineer.

As ever in cases like these, there are questions as yet unanswered. What happened to Reg's DCM recommendation? Why is there no sign of a commission after he had obviously spent some time in England in officer training? All in all a tremendous tale and an indication of what is possible with a little initial primary evidence and a lot of online sleuthing.

17

HUGHIE CAIRNS: A
FOOTBALLER'S TALE

I n 1911, Hughie Cairns and his family left Ashington, Northumberland in north-east England for Saskatoon, Saskatchewan in Canada. Hughie was 14 years old. At 16 and 18 he was hailed as one of the best young soccer players in the country. At 21 he died of wounds in hospital on the Western Front, wounds gained in a brave action that earned him a Victoria Cross and a very special and permanent place in Canadian history. His own story starts back in the coalfields of Victorian Northumberland.

Hugh Cairns was born in December 1896, the third son of Northumbrian George Cairns and his Durham-born wife Elizabeth. Hugh's grandfather had moved south from Scotland and worked as an agricultural labourer in various parts of Northumberland before settling down in the coalfield at Bilton Banks near Shilbottle. Hugh's father worked as a coal miner here and, after marriage, moved to Ashington. At the time of the 1901 census, young Hughie was living with his parents at 59 Seventh Row Ashington, one of six children. If the house numbering remains unaltered, the home is still there today. By 1911, there were eleven children in the family. Father was a deputy overman and Hugh had started work in the colliery processing department.

Soon after the 1911 census, the family moved to Canada where Hughie immediately made his mark as a soccer player. The side he captained won the local league in 1913 and he was in another side which triumphed in 1915. By then he had begun an apprenticeship as a plumber but on 2 August 1915 he enlisted in the Canadian army. He was now 18.

By June 1916, Hughie was back in England where he was transferred to the 46th Battalion. By early August he was in France and soon showed the kind of determination and leadership that must have been apparent on the football pitch. On 11 August 1917, he was given a stripe. A fortnight later he was awarded the Distinguished Conduct Medal (DCM). The citation for this reads:

> Awarded DCM for conspicuous gallantry and devotion to unit in leading a party forwards at a critical moment and supplying covering fire to the flank of an attacking Battalion. With great initiative he recovered two guns which had been left behind [and loaded them] repelling three enemy attacks and successfully covering our subsequent withdrawal. Though wounded he held on until all his ammunition was expended, when he made his way back to our line having done invaluable service and set a very fine example.

This action took place earlier in the summer of 1917 and he suffered a number of shrapnel wounds in his back. In July 1918, he was promoted to corporal and in August to sergeant. By November

1918, he was at the gates of the French city of Valenciennes after taking part in every one of the battalion's major actions since coming to France. On 2 November, shortly after the surrender of Austria, Hugh Cairns died of wounds received in the attack which had been made on the city during the previous day. He was awarded a posthumous Victoria Cross. The citation reads:

> For most conspicuous bravery before Valenciennes on 1 November 1918, when a machine gun opened on his platoon. Without a moment's hesitation, Sergeant Cairns seized a Lewis gun and single-handedly, in the face of direct fire, rushed the post, killed the crew of five, and captured the gun. Later, when the line was held up by machine-gun fire, he again rushed forward, killing 12 enemy soldiers and capturing another 18 and two guns. Subsequently, when the advance was held up by machine guns and field guns, although wounded, he led a small party to outflank them, killing many, forcing about 50 to surrender, and capturing all of the guns. After consolidation, he went with a battle patrol to exploit Marly and forced 60 enemy soldiers to surrender. Whilst disarming the party he was severely wounded. Nevertheless, he opened fire and inflicted heavy losses. Finally he was rushed by about 20 enemy soldiers and collapsed from weakness and loss of blood. Throughout the operation he showed the highest degree of valour, and his leadership contributed to the success of the attack.

Those who have written about him after the event suggest that he was spurred on by the loss in action of his brother Albert who had died at Cambrai in September 1918. Albert, also Northumbrian by birth, was buried at Terlinchun British Cemetery in Pas de Calais while Hugh's body lies in Auberchicourt British Cemetery, 7km east of Douai, near Nord, France. The well-known Canadian general Arthur Currie referred to Hugh Cairns' effort as a 'superhuman deed'.

Since his death, Hugh Cairns has become a symbol for all Canadian soccer players who gave their lives in battle. In 1921, a statue of him in soccer kit was unveiled in Saskatoon's Kiwanis Park. Around the base are the names of other Canadian soccer players who gave their lives. A representation of this statue appears on shirts and medals and is the focus for Remembrance Day ceremonies. His valour is also remembered in a plaque outside the family home, a street name in Valenciennes, a street and school name in Saskatoon and a regimental armoury.

Research Tip: Take Care with Indexes

Progress is a wonderful thing yet it would be churlish to criticise volunteers who spent hour after hour in past years transcribing names onto index lists and, from time to time, 'getting them wrong'. Take, for example, the surname of war hero Hughie Cairns and its appearance in more than one census research engine as 'Cavins'. At a first glance at the digitised census entries for the family, it is easy to see how the error has been made. When the entry is 'blown up' in a digitised version, the name Cairns is much easier to make out. As it appears to the naked eye on the original, the surname does look like Cavins. Most of those who became involved in active service during the First World War will appear on the 1901 and 1911 censuses and a large number on two or three censuses from earlier dates too. Compared to the censuses of the early nineteenth century, the quality of the enumerators' presentation has generally improved, making it easier to spot people. Some of the indexes, however, still predate digitisation. The Cairns family was eventually discovered via the address search engine available on the Genealogist website and prior knowledge of family Christian names and birthplaces.

THE TALE BEHIND THE TALE

I came across the story of Hugh Cairns completely out of the blue while judging a song competition at the Morpeth Gathering in Northumberland some five years ago. One fine entry composed by Northumbrian Tom Patterson had Hughie's name for its title. The main drift of the text was that Ashington had a locally born hero who seemed to have been ignored, mainly because the family had emigrated. As I was writing for a Northumbrian magazine at the time and realised that most of the online material about the hero came mainly from Canada and dealt with his Canadian and war years, I decided to do a little local sleuthing myself. According to one Canadian website, Hugh was born in 'Ashington, Newcastle-on-Tyne, England', which is approximate enough for those living far from his birth-place. Ashington actually lies 15 to 20 miles to the north of the

---

HUGHIE CAIRNS.   Tom Patterson (Class B1 2006)

"Come me lads, now let's get cracking
Pack your bags we'll be off soon.
The pit head here will be a memory
When we reach Saskatoon."
And so it was in Canada that he came to make his name
As a sportsman and a leading light in the English football game

Who knows where this world will lead us?
Who knows how the dice will fall?
Hughie Cairns was on life's journey
Following his call

But the clouds of war were growing
"Show your mettle, have your say.
Come and serve the British Empire
Sign up here today."
And so two brothers dressed in brown marched past St Thomas School
With the cheers still ringing in their ears they were bound for Liverpool.

Words of Hughie Cairns' song.

city of Newcastle upon Tyne beyond the city bounds and in the county of Northumberland.

At first, I was a little surprised that nothing much appears to have been done on his Northumbrian roots but this may be explained by the mistransription of the Cairns family name as Cavins, as already mentioned. The story of Hugh's early years as told in the main tale is thus based on what has been discovered by bypassing these indexes.

The relevant War Diary (46th Battalion),proves useful in working out exactly what happened on the day of his death:

> We captured 3 field guns, one trench mortar, 7 machine guns and over fifty prisoners and the ground had plenty of dead on it. The advance then continued to the south edge of the factory without much opposition. Here I ordered Sergt Cairns with 8 other ranks and 1 L.A.R. to seize the railway crossing in E.16.c.85.30 … Lieut. MacLeod left 7 O.R.'s in the houses while he and Sergt Cairns and 2 O.R's with L.A.R. proceeded to examine factory, Sergt Cairns handling the gun himself. Just as they were crossing the street a Boshe opened on them with an automatic rifle. Sergt Cairns made a run for the swinging door opening into the court-yard shooting his L.A.R. from the hip. Those he did not kill or wound ran down a back street. At this time Lieut. MacLeod and one O.R. entered the courtyard and as they proceeded around the corner they discovered about 50 more Boshe in a passage in a south-easterly end of the yard. Here they ordered them to put up their hands which was done immediately with the exception of one Boshe who retained his rifle. Lieut. MacLeod immediately covered him with his revolver when a Boshe Officer made a motion as if to put the rifle aside at the same time drew his pistol and shot Sergt Cairns through the stomach. Sergt Cairns then opened fire from the hip killing and wounding about 30. The Boshe then saw they must fight for their lives and com-

menced firing a machine gun from a high brick wall. Sergt Cairns was again hit through the wrist but continued to fire his L.A.R. when he finally got a bullet through his hand nearly taking it off. This bullet also broke the L.A.R. He then threw the L.A.R. in the face of one of the Boshe who were firing at him, knocking him over. He then staggered to the gateway and collapsed. He was being carried back to our line when M.G. fire opened from the left killing one of the carrying party. Lieut. MacLeod then dragged him into our lines.

R.W. Gyles Capt.
C.C. "A" Company (O.R. = other rank)

There is also further online information on what happened after Hughie Cairns's death. Although the statue is of Hughie, the base contains the names of seventy-five footballers from Saskatoon who were killed during the war. In the 1970s, the Cairns family donated all the family medals to the armoury named after Hugh, although the Victoria Cross is now on display at the Canadian War Museum in Ottawa. A couple of decades later, the provincial government decided to put a plaque up outside the family home but managed to trace the wrong Hugh Cairns. In 2005, this error was rectified and the plaque is now on display outside the correct address. (A useful cautionary tale for family researchers – Hugh Cairns does not sound a familiar name but there were at least two of them in Saskatoon about the time of the First World War. Never take an 'unusual' name for granted!)

In years to come, Hugh's 'home town' was to produce a series of soccer greats in the form of the Charlton brothers and Jackie Milburn and it is fitting that Hughie himself is now remembered in song.

18

TOM CRAWFORD: AN ENTERTAINER'S TALE

Tom Crawford was born into a shipyard family in Clydebank, Scotland in 1887. In his youth, he spent some time in the south west of England where his father had moved for work. Later the family went back to Scotland and Tom too began to work in the shipyards. However he was drawn elsewhere by the smell of greasepaint and the bright lights of the theatre and in the years immediately before the war, he was leading man in a Scottish play that visited all the top 'minor' theatres in Britain. At the outbreak of war, he was in America, working the music halls in a sketch with a Scottish comedian and developing his own musical comedy act.

The war eventually brought Tom back to Britain and he found work in what he described as a 'gun shop' in Glasgow. Here he was in charge of the stores where the barrels for howitzers and other weapons were loaded for distribution. When his call-up papers came, he was summoned to Stirling Castle where an officer asked if he had any trade. For some peculiar reason he said he was a carpenter although, on his own admission later in life, his carpentry skills were rather limited. He was put to the test and asked to dovetail some pieces of wood. As this was about the limit of his carpentry skills, he passed the test. When asked where he would like to work as a carpenter, he said the Royal Flying Corps, as to him that sounded the most inviting of military organisations.

Tom's first posting was to 27 Training Squadron near London and his first task was to build an office for the flight sergeant. He did so and the hut immediately collapsed. The Training Squadron was a relatively small unit and Tom was happy here. although on one occasion he was ordered to help in clearing up after one of the training planes had crashed into a tree and burst into flames. The poor pilot had been burned to a crisp and the memory of the incident remained with Tom for the rest of his life.

While Tom was with the 27th, the officer in command decided to try to improve morale by arranging some entertainment. At one parade time, the flight sergeant enquired if there were any entertainers in the squadron and asked them to stand forward. According to Tom, all but half a dozen volunteered, safe in the knowledge that life would probably be made easier for them. It soon became clear that 'Crawford', as he was known, had professional experience in the field and within a short time he had set up a concert party called Flying Frolics. Eventually he was summoned to the flight sergeant's office (he must have found a real carpenter to build him one), and was told that the success of his concert party had attracted 'the bigger squadrons'. Would he like to move on? Tom turned down the offer as it was for him personally and he would have to completely rebuild a new concert party.

From London, Tom moved to Aldershot for a few weeks. He was not happy here as a great deal of 'square bashing' was involved and this had not been the case in the more relaxed atmosphere of a small training camp. His next port of call was Farnborough where there was an important RAF establishment (and the RFC had become the RAF by the time he was there). At one point Tom was 'away in the wilds' at Perham Down, which the Australians used during the war for training. Here he became involved in work on improving the canteen. The canteen had a piano and as one of the men started to play, Tom began to sing. He was greeted with an encore and eventually set up a concert party here too. This party had 'a fine tenor' and a conjuror.

Tom's final posting was to Driffield in East Yorkshire 'towards the end of the war'. Here he was with No. 21 Training Depot. According to one website this was 'the first aerodrome to occupy the site' and was 'made up of wooden and brick buildings, similar to those found at Duxford or Hendon'. The airfield was set up in 1918 and, trusting that Tom's carpentry skills had now improved, seems to have been the kind of place to which he might have been sent. He was demobbed from Driffield and, like many others, was provided with a demob suit but when interviewed at the age of 90 was unable to recall what it was like.

THE TALE BEHIND THE TALE

Tom Crawford's tale is stunningly different from many of the others in the book and serves as a reminder that for many the war was rarely dangerous or glorious. 'Old Tom', as I knew him, was an entertainer for most of his life. My father first came across him when Tom was approaching his 90th year and living in a nursing home in Carlisle. He had spent most of his life as an entertainer, often experiencing long periods without work. Although his career as a comedian had not been massively successful, it had seen him performing in the theatre, in films and on both radio and television, and he was known to many a household name. Towards the end of his life he caused quite a stir when he appeared on Hughie Green's TV talent show *Opportunity Knocks* where he sang the tear-jerking 'My Old Dutch'. My father spent hours recording him on tapes, tapes that are in my possession today and gradually being digitised.

During the Second World War, Tom travelled with ENSA, the forces entertainment body. There was no such organisation during the First World War but it is clear that Tom did his best to 'rally the troops' by organising entertainment. In fact, he claims on the tape that he was one of the founders of this kind of forces' entertainment as he knew of few other named concert parties formed during that period. When Tom died in 1980, he left my father a suitcase full of memorabilia. This too is now in my possession and is a little treasure trove of books, scripts, photographs and posters that chronicle the life of a small-time wandering entertainer.

Unfortunately from the point of view of the current work, there is little relating to his wartime activities among his memorabilia. His tale comes from listening to his memories on tape, recorded in September 1977 when he was 90. However, the two relevant pieces of wartime memorabilia that have survived are still of considerable interest.

The first of the two pieces is a photograph of Tom in his RFC uniform, taken, according to a stamp on the back, at Colwyn Bay. Useful as this is, it is a few written words on the back that gives the photograph real value. These read 'Best wishes, parson – Elisabeth Welch'. The provenance of this signature is fascinating too. Elisabeth Welch was a well-known American singer and actress of stage and screen in the 1930s. She was up alongside Crosby and Sinatra, had 'Stormy Weather' as her theme tune

and duetted famously with Paul Robeson in a successful musical film of the 1930s. In the Second World War she toured with
ENSA and Tom revealed, in interview, that his act was the one
that preceded hers when they were on tour. At the time, Tom's
most successful comedy sketch featured him as a Scottish parson

Picture of Tom Crawford, signed on the back by Elisabeth Welch.

Tom Crawford's RFC armband.

reading out notices from the pulpit and getting them hilariously muddled. ('Drink is man's worst enemy' and 'treat your enemy as you would a friend' for example!) He must have produced the photograph of himself as an old 'soldier' (or airman) in the previous conflict and asked the star to sign it. Elisabeth Welch's contributions to ENSA are noted in a history of the company published in the late twentieth century.

The other piece of memorabilia is what looks at first glance like an RFC armband. Stamped on it is the lettering RFC and two sets of numbers, 19318 and 101636. On the reverse side of the 'armband' are three little sleeve pockets with a small tuck in pocket at the bottom. Could this be part of the equipment used by a joiner or air mechanic – a little cloth toolkit for screwdrivers etc? It was only while writing this book that I decided to explore further.

As the book was being completed a third helpmeet turned up as a salutary reminder to double-check all resources before abandoning them. Having come across a few pages of handwritten script from around the period he was in the forces, I turned the sheets over to discover that the script had been written out on the reverse sides of pieces of headed notepaper. 'Tam' Crawford, they declared at the top, was (or had been) Principal Comedian

Royal Air Force Concert Party 21 T D S Driffield, Yorks, and Principal Comedian Royal Air Force Concert Party FLYING FROLICS 27 Training Squadron, London Colney. This information helped to tie up some of the tale's loose ends.

The rather grand claims made on the headed paper were very much in line with Tom's expansive and determined character. Nevertheless, placed alongside the relevant tapes and memorabilia, they were very useful in telling Tom's story. His war was a relatively quiet one but it must have been thus for many employed in useful yet unexciting occupations. Such people still had a tale worthy of the telling.

19

ARTIE WATTERSON: A SUBMARINER'S TALE

Thomas Arthur 'Artie' Watterson was born in Liverpool in 1891 and spent his younger working life in the merchant navy, working his way through his mate's and master's tickets up to 1912. He was 5ft 8in tall with a fresh complexion, dark hair and brown eyes and had two scars on his ankle. After an apprenticeship out of Liverpool, he served as a deck officer on a couple of Sunderland-registered ships working out of Liverpool – the *Cedar Branch* and the *Elm Branch*. He later worked in other vessels up to the outbreak of war. He was also an officer in the Royal Naval Reserve (RNR) and one of over 200 officers in the RNR to serve in submarines during the First World War.

Unlike a number of young men featured in this book, Artie was involved in the war from day one. In fact he had joined the RNR as a probationary sub-lieutenant a month before the war started. Within weeks he had finished preparations and was on board submarine E2 patrolling the German and Dutch coast. He remained in submarines for his entire wartime career. His early career was spent in submarine E2 during its involvement in the Gallipoli campaign. Thanks to a submariner's diary that has survived from this period we know that E2 was busy through-out the campaign, moving around a great deal, bombing Turkish defences and sinking small sailing vessels that were thought to be helping the enemy.

During the First World War, groups of submarines were attached to individual warships and E2 started with HMS *Maidstone* then moved through HMS *Adamant* to HMS *Europa* stationed in Malta. In the summer of 1916, Artie moved to Blyth just north of Newcastle upon Tyne, and to a brand new prestigious submarine J4 under the protection of HMS *Talisman*. By January 1918, he was lieutenant on board submarine K4 and destined for the most unfortunate of ends. On 31 January a fleet of warships and submarines headed out of the Firth of Forth for exercises in the North Sea. The weather conditions were poor and in the confusion that arose as a result, the cruiser HMS *Fearless* collided with the first in the column of submarines. The submarines that were following began to make efforts to avoid the stricken submarine and the K4, upon which Artie was serving, was struck by two other submarines. One of these collisions nearly cut K4 in two. The submarine sank and the entire crew was lost. The same was the case with the lead submarine, K17.

Black humour caused this catastrophe, which was responsible for the loss of over 100 lives, to be named 'The Battle of May Island' after a small island in the Firth. Much of the detail was glossed over until the release of relevant papers towards the end of the twentieth century. Even as the fleet had sailed out, the K class of submarines already had a poor reputation which had earned them the nickname 'Kalamity Class'. Prior to its final demise, the

K4 had been grounded off the west coast of England and had collided with another K class submarine off the coast of Denmark.

By the time of his death, Artie Watterson had been awarded a medal for his distinguished service in submarines. In any war, submarine service is acknowledged to be one of the most dangerous occupations, as a hit or collision of any kind underwater was likely to lead to the death of all on board. Artie had survived for all but ten months of a lengthy conflict only to die as a result of a most bizarre form of friendly fire. He was, according to official records, 'discharged dead' on 31 January 1918 and his name is one of over fifty on the official K4 memorial in St Margaret Patten's church East Cheap, London.

THE TALE BEHIND THE TALE

This sad tale came as a result of another serendipitous meeting. When my nephew (the great-grandson of 'Fred Stephens' – chapter one), was getting married, I fell into conversation with the bride's Aunt Alison on the subject of our shared interest in family history. I explained that I was just embarking on a book of case studies on the First World War and Alison said that she 'might have something of interest' from her own family. Little did I realise what a treasure trove was about to head in my direction.

The package, when it arrived by post, contained carefully organised copies of photographs, press cuttings, letters, potted histories and lengthy histories plus merchant navy and Royal Navy records. From all these, it was possible to piece together not only the dramatic story of Artie's wartime activity but indeed a complete picture of his life at work and war.

Artie's pre-war career was covered by a variety of certificates of discharge and apprenticeship linked to vessels in which he served, as well as comments on his ability and character from various ship masters. (The mark was invariably V.G.) There were also a number of written references from master mariners under whom he had served and the owners of shipping companies for which he worked. The certificates of competency and attached documents listing vessels served in (now on view at www.ancestry.com) proved useful in completing the picture of his pre-war activities. There were also family photographs and photographs of vessels in which he served during this period.

The records of his service during the war are also very full. Many of them were forwarded to Alison from or via the Royal Navy Submarine Museum. With the submarine a fairly new weapon of war at the time and the submariners relatively few in number, the interest in research had been considerable over the years. This is especially true of officers and officers like Artie Watterson who had a reputation for being one of the finest officers in the service. His service record forwarded from here is

5. The Battle of May Island

The K class . . . have been successful vessels. . . . In fleet exercises they always fulfilled the functions for which they were designed.—Submarine Administration, Training and Construction, published by the Technical History Section of the Admiralty, 1921.

The only good thing about K boats was that they never engaged the enemy. — Rear-Admiral Ernest W. Leir, R.N. (retd.), in an interview, February 1961.

IN December of 1917 Vice-Admiral Beatty moved his K boats from Scapa Flow to Rosyth, believing that they would be better placed tactically in the Forth estuary.

Read around the subject.

Artie Watterson with his family. (Alison Harris)

very full. His name also appears in the annual navy lists running from 1914 to 1917.

The Battle of May Island and the history of submarine warfare in the First World War are dealt with at length in a number of books and on a number of online sites.

Online searches bring up his name in the Portsmouth Memorial Register and also the names of his parents, John and Clara. John was a port pilot at Liverpool so the sea was in Artie's blood. The register also shows that Artie was married to Marian and was 27 at the time of his death. His probate was proved at Chester in April 1918 and involved William Herbert Robinson, foreign correspondent and step relative. Artie's estate was valued at just over £387. There are also online accounts of modern underwater visits to the wreck of the E2. Family photographs from this period show Artie in uniform and include a modern picture of the E2 memorial at St Margaret Patten's church, East Cheap. There are also photographs of some of the submarines upon which he served.

Artie Watterson was Alison's maternal grandfather.

20

WILKINSON, LUCAS, TIDDY AND BUTTERWORTH: THE MORRIS DANCERS' TALE

The first decade of the twentieth century saw a revival of interest in traditional morris dancing. Musician Cecil Sharp collected a number of these dances from various old dancers and musicians, mainly from the villages of the Cotswolds, and formed a team of seven young men (six dancers and a reserve). The idea was to take the dances around the country in order to recreate interest. The young men involved were academics and musicians themselves and this tale involves four of them.

GEORGE JERRARD WILKINSON (1885–1916)

George Wilkinson's main profession was a teacher of music. He had succeeded Cecil Sharp as the music master at Ludgrove, one of Eton's prep schools. Sharp said that he was a 'good teacher' and a beautiful dancer. George was born in Birmingham in 1885, the son of a Leicestershire vicar and a Gloucestershire mother. He was with his parents at census time in 1891 and at Uppingham School ten years later. After studying at Caius College, Cambridge, where he held musical scholarships, he took up an interest in song writing and traditional music and dance. He was in his mid-twenties when he became involved in Sharp's demonstration dance side.

During the First World War, George became a sergeant signaller in the Duke of Cambridge's Own (Middlesex Regiment) 16th Battalion. He served in France from November 1915 and was killed during the attack on Beaumont Hamel on 1 July 1916, the dread first day of the Somme campaign. He had joined the public schools' battalion during the first year of the war and his name and brief biography both feature in De Ruvigny's Roll of Honour. His address at the time of his death was Sutton in Surrey.

PERCIVAL DREWETT LUCAS (1879–1916)

Percival Lucas died five days after his fellow morris man. He was the younger brother of the writer and essayist E.V. Lucas. Born into a wealthy Sussex family in 1879, he was able to lead the life of a gentleman and married locally in 1907. Lucas became interested in the Edwardian revival of traditional dance and was active, with Sharp, in the formation of the English Folk Dance Society in 1911. In the census of that year he was described as an 'antiquarian author and record agent'. He then edited the first two editions of the prestigious academic *Folk Music Journal* (still published annually and highly regarded in academic circles today).

As a member of Sharp's dance side, Percy was reckoned to be the most enthusiastic and energetic of dancers and one who appreciated what the folk dance revival was all about. According to his war records, after brief service in the 21st Royal Fusiliers, he joined the Border Regiment as a private late in May 1916 and was soon at the front. He gained approval for a commission in June and was swiftly promoted to second lieutenant in the 2nd Battalion of the Border Regiment. On 6 July 1916, he died of wounds suffered on the Somme. He was buried in Abbeville Cemetery. His next of kin is noted on his record as Mrs P.D. Lucas, Greatham, Pulborough, Sussex, an address which has been amended (by hand) to 92, Brook Street (London) W6.

Percy Lucas and his wife were said to have been known to the author D.H. Lawrence and used as templates for characters in one of his works, where both were painted in a rather unflattering manner. It has since been noted that the author felt guilty of this portrayal when he learnt of the dancer's untimely end.

REGINALD JOHN ELLIOTT TIDDY (1880–1916)

Reg Tiddy died on 10 August 1916. He was born in Margate in 1880 and his father, a Cornishman, was described as a tutor on the 1881 census; his mother came from Oxfordshire. Reg went to Tonbridge School and was a scholar at Oxford in 1901. A year later, he was awarded a prize fellowship and his fascination with Anglo-Saxon history led to an interest in other English traditions and, like Sharp, he became an enthusiastic collector. His home was at Ascott Under Wychwood, a village known for its own traditional morris dances. He acted as reserve for the travelling morris side.

During the war, Reg joined the 4th Battalion of the Oxfordshire and Buckinghamshire Light Infantry and was commissioned as a lieutenant. He first saw action in France in May 1916 and was killed on 10 August 1916, apparently while searching trenches for wounded soldiers. A brief biography states that he was 'killed instantly by a shell'. His grave can be found in the British military cemetery at Laventie, midway between Béthune and Armentières.

Reg Tiddy's *Collection of Mummers' Plays* was published post-humously in 1923 and is considered to be the first academic collection of real value on this fascinating topic. A modern mumming enthusiast visited Tiddy's grave in 2008 and wrote a piece on him for the Master Mummers' website.

GEORGE SAINTON KAYE BUTTERWORTH (1885–1916)

George Butterworth was born on 12 July 1885 in Paddington. A self-declared cockney by birth he was brought up 'in the spirit of Yorkshire' where he spent some of his formative years. He attended Eton and appears on the 1901 census there on the same page as John Maynard Keynes. He moved on to Trinity, Oxford and then tried teaching. After this, he decided to concentrate on musical composition and to that end attended the Royal College of Music.

Like Sharp and contemporary Vaughan Williams, Butterworth was fascinated by traditional music and dance. He was part of the original English Folk Dance Society Committee of 1911 and travelled with Sharp as he collected sword dances in Yorkshire. He helped Sharp to put together one of his famed morris dance books and is held responsible for the noting down of the popular morris dances from Badby in Northamptonshire. He also danced in Sharp's side.

Butterworth joined the Duke of Cornwall's Light Infantry early in the war and served with merit. A commissioned officer, he was shot by a sniper at Pozières on the same day that Reginald Tiddy was killed. His body was never recovered and his name appears on the Thiepval Memorial. He was awarded a Military Cross and also had a trench named after him. In the world of music, he is best known for his musical setting of A.E. Houseman's *A Shropshire Lad*.

THE TALE BEHIND THE TALE

Morris dancers are unwelcome prophets in their own country, or so, with over fifty years' personal experience as a morris dancer, it seems to me. On the one extreme they are portrayed as overweight, lumbering, bearded boozers and at the other as rather effeminate and balletic 'hankie wavers' and all this being compounded by arguments over the role of women in the tradition. This is rarely the case outside England where the dancers and their dances are greeted with great enthusiasm. All of this is possibly an unnecessary rant but one essential to an understanding of the inclusion in the book of this final case study.

Photographs of the morris dance side covered in the study show its dancing style to have fallen into the latter category. With few exceptions, traditional morris dancing of the stick and handkerchief variety had disappeared over a vast swathe of rural England. Sharp is credited with reviving the art after witnessing a side perform at Headington Quarry near Oxford at Christmas 1899, and the side he formed was of young men who were fit and danced with elegance. The tale of the demise of Sharp's side in a single year is known among the morris dance community and has attracted increased attention within recent years. The tale of each man comes from a variety of sources. Some of the information was already online as at least two of them are still remembered for their contributions to the revival of folk tradition. The rest was filled in from the usual sources used in researching a soldier from the First World War. As this book was being written, a blue plaque was being put in place in memory of one of the dancers.

As noted on a number of occasions in this book, the true horror of a war like the First World War is often best brought home by reference to the experience of individuals or small groups of individuals. My interest in sporting history, for example, has often brought me to post-war rugby and cricket teams devastated by the First World War. Not only were they affected by the loss of those who never returned but also by the failure of many wounded in body and spirit who were now unable to play the games they loved. In the case of rugby in Sunderland, for example, this dramatic loss led to a massive campaign to involve youngsters in the game under the auspices of the local club, the education authority and the shipyard owners. All this is placed in perspective by an experience I had just after leaving teaching. In 2006, I was invited to visit the Somme for a week in order to write an article for a popular family history magazine. At one military cemetery, the excellent English guide showed us the graves of a 'David Beckham', an 'Ian Botham' a 'Beethoven' and a 'future prime minister'; all young men with futures before the conflict.

We forget how fortunate we are at our peril.

Research Tip: What to Look Out For

This book has no summary at the end; all lies in the individual cases. However, there are some global points which are worth mentioning:

- The Somme is flagged up regularly as a major event, and rightly so; yet the consequences of the German push of 1918 in terms of casualties and POWs must be equally noteworthy.
- Soldiers were killed and wounded in action but others died or became severely disabled on active service on account of living conditions to which they were unaccustomed.
- The fog of war, accidents and friendly fire all rear their ugly heads on numerous occasions in a way which must be familiar to those who have seen action but less so to those who have not.

Above all, the evidence is that, despite the passing of all adults who took an active part in the First World War, there is much in the way of material out there to enable the dedicated researcher to reconstruct the lives and experiences of 'those who served'.

INDEX

Abbeville 24, 84, 184

Aldershot 73, 104, 106, 109, 171

Alexandria 21

Anzac 16

Anzac Cove 22, 23, 77

Armentieres 24–5, 185

Arras, Battle of 16, 110, 112–13, 115

Ashington 162-3, 166

Avonmouth 21, 27

Bailleul 25

Barrow–in-Furness 20, 29, 62, 67, 78–9

Bayne, Sandy 23–4, 28–9, 99

Bedford 27

Bedfords (Regiment) 135

Bisley 20

Blandford 63, 73

Bletchley 24

Boulogne 27, 160

Brookwood 20

Bulford Camp 20, 55

Cairo 21

Calais 41, 164

Cambrai, Battle of 16, 18, 26, 164

Cambridge 76, 150, 152, 155, 183

Cape Helles 21

Carlisle 8, 12, 103–4, 106, 144, 171

Cassel 24

Catterick 27

Chatham 70, 74

Chelmsford 118–19, 122, 131, 133

Churchill 15

Dover 41, 51, 54, 129

Dranoutre 25

Durban 56. 59

Duston 85, 86, 100

Franconia, SS 21, 27

Freiburg 35–6

Gallipoli 8, 15, 18, 21–2, 27, 29, 32, 77–80, 92, 99, 146, 177

George V, King 20

Gibraltar 21

Good Easter 125, 131, 133–4

Ham 34–5

Harlesden 20

Harris, Alison 13, 178–9, 181

Haverigg 55, 103, 104

Haveringcourt 26

Hindenburg Line 26, 133

Jutland, Battle of 16

Kildonian Castle, SS 24

King's Lynn 76, 78–80

Krithia 21

KSLI 83–5, 87, 89–90. 93, 97,

Le Havre 24

Lemnos 21, 24

Letitia, SS 24

Liverpool 9, 33, 37, 42, 47, 49, 50–1, 53–4, 74, 176, 180,

Lone Pine 22

Loos, Battle of 16

Malta 21, 24, 27, 177

Manchester 27

Marne, Battle of 15, 16

Mary, Queen 20

May Island, Battle of 177, 180

Messines, Battle of 16, 18, 25, 32, 140

Millom 9, 10, 19-20, 23, 29, 32–3, 41, 47, 49, 51, 54–5, 105, 107

Monk, Richard 121–2, 126–7, 129

Mons, Battle of 16, 82

morris dancing 13, 182–6

Nek, The 22

Netley 24

Newport Pagnell 24

Norfolk and Norfolks 76–82, 119, 122

Oswestry 63, 66, 101
Oxford 184–6

Parchim 129, 131
Passchendaele, Battle of 16, 18
Portsmouth 70, 85, 96, 180
Pozières 134, 185

Red Cross (International)
    48–9, 53, 129, 131, 146
Redmond, Captain 26
Royal Air Force (RAF) 9, 15,
    63, 65, 67, 83, 155, 171, 175
Royal Flying Corps (RFC) 9,
    12, 15, 63, 65, 67, 170–2, 174
Roxwell 118, 121, 131,

St Austell 20
St Quentin 33, 54
Salisbury 20
Saskatoon 162, 165, 168
Seang-Bee 21
Sharp, Cecil 182-186
Shrewsbury 84, 91, 95, 97–8.
    101
Skipper, Joe 151, 160–1
Snaefell, SS 21

Somme, Battle of 8, 12, 16,
    69, 72, 75, 84, 134, 151, 160,
    183–4, 187–8
South Africa 11, 59, 105, 110,
    113–4, 116,
Strasbourg 35, 54
Suvla Bay 22–4, 77, 80

Tamar Valley 20
Truro 20

Valenciennes 164–5
Verdun, Battle of 16

Wembley 20
Winchcombe 83, 85, 94, 97,
    101-2
Woking 20, 104, 108–9, 112
Wulgerham 25

Yate 66, 67
YMCA 45, 57, 60, 90
Ypres, Battle of 16, 18, 25–6,
    31, 84, 92, 119, 138, 140,
    143–4, 146

Zeebrugge 17

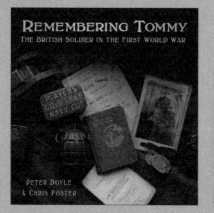

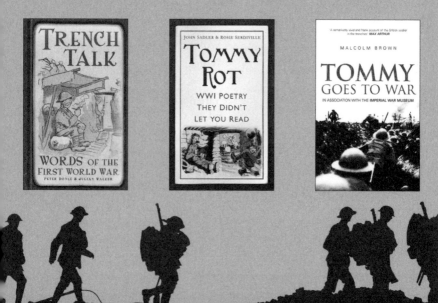